MW01028873

In Her Father's Footsteps

With the 90th *Normandy to the Moselle, 1944*

Chris Johnston

Copyright © 2016 by Chris Johnston

Dedicated to the men of Company A, 1st Battalion, 358th Regiment, of the 90th Division.

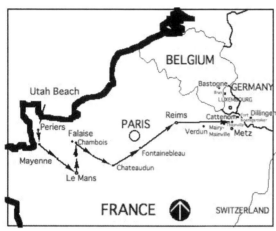

BATTLE ROUTE OF THE 90TH INFANTRY DIVISION
6 JUNE - 12 SEPTEMBER 1944

Contents

Introduction

" Those were days I will always remember. It was an honor to lead men of "A" Company. They were wonderful soldiers and performed well under terrible conditions. "

Col H.C. Neil in October 1992

I was introduced to my future father in law in the fall of 1975. His gun cabinet was a treasure trove full of guns brought back from WWII. A framed set of medals hung quietly on a side hall wall placed there by his insistent and devoted wife. Eventually, I read a newspaper article that discussed a captured tank column involving Lt. Harris Neil from Dallas, Texas so I thought I had a decent idea about the origin of his medals.

Like most veterans ,that saw combat, he did not volunteer discussion about the war. I did not know the questions to ask and his children never heard him speak about details of the war. I learned a bit listening at the family deer camp late at night in Menard, Texas. Occasionally, his contemporaries would ask him questions and there would be a story here or there. I heard him discuss an explosion at a fort where he was burned and where there were Germans flying out in the air from the explosion, but it was only a bit here and there and not very detailed.

While we were all freezing our tails off sitting around a campfire in sub-freezing weather wearing every available item of clothing, he would be sitting next to the fire in a light jacket. When you asked him if he wanted more clothes, the reply would be that he was acclimated. He had been acclimated in the arctic conditions of the Battle of the Bulge. The truth was that he had nerve damage and never felt the cold. We would all have to watch his booted feet at the edge of the fire because he would often catch fire and never feel it. He said he had never ever felt cold again after surviving the Battle of the Bulge.

I shot my first deer at that camp in 1975 with an M1 carbine serial # 2881416 loaned to me by my future father-in-law. After his death, we became stewards of that gun. Research of Lt. Neil's diary entries indicates that he carried that M1 in WWII. Gradually, we started to know more details about his war from his personal effects and started gathering information over about a ten-year period. The more we learned, the more we yearned to know. The idea for a trip to follow his WWII unit through France started to percolate. His diary was the starting point. Researched information was overlaid with the diary information. Places were identified and a trip itinerary was finally in place.

We drove through France in the summer of 2014 on a pilgrimage to shadow his unit's path during his time in the war. This book is my weak attempt to honor and document all that we have learned about H.C. Neil and what he experienced during WWII.

Chapter One

BUTCH

"I know that I shall never forget what took place over there, but it's very hard to try and tell anyone about it. I never realized that people knew so little about what actually took place. "

Letter from Carl Weingartner to Lt. H.C. Neil, 9 Dec. 1945

H.C. Neil Jr. was called "Butch or "Neil "by most of his close friends. Everyone nagged him to put his memoirs on paper. He was a diligent record keeper and photographer. Like Thomas Jefferson, he logged the annual production of his back-yard tomatoes and apple trees and kept up to date military 201 files on his children that were turned over to them upon marriage as they transferred to their new outfits. It looks like he did try to write the war experience down on paper twice about twenty years apart. Both attempts cover a lot of the pre-combat experience, but they stop there. And at the deer camp, he would talk on and on about the good times during his post war occupation experience. He was just not really ready to discuss his combat experience.

Brothers Frank and Harris C. Neil Jr.

It is impossible to do justice to this story without first hand experience. In one of Butch's memoir starts, he states " It is quite impossible to put the actual feelings, thoughts, fears, etc. down on paper for others to read and feel in some way the same emotions without first hand knowledge. He goes on to state that he believed his experiences were probably average for an infantry officer. "

Harris Claude Neil Jr. was born May 8, 1916 in Fort Valley, Georgia. His father, Harris Claude Neil was a Vice President and comptroller for Coca Cola and with his wife, Maud Miller Neil and family migrated to Dallas in the 1920's. In an early patriotic childhood picture, Butch is pictured in a Navy uniform while his big brother Frank was outfitted in Army garb. Both would later proudly serve their country, but they would swap uniforms as adults. Ironically, Frank would serve in the Navy while Butch, who would never ever learn to swim joined the Army. Ironically, there would be an abundance of time on the water in his future.

At Highland Park High School in Dallas, Texas, Butch joined the R.O.T.C. and rose to the highest level as the Cadet regimental commander. Lt. Neil received his commission as a second lieutenant in the Army reserve in 1937. After finishing his studies at S.M.U. in the summer of 1941, he was called to active duty in November 1941 as a Testing and Training Officer and Company Commander at Camp Wolters near Mineral Wells, Texas. He felt confident in his abilities because he had spent three summers on maneuvers with the Texas National Guard and four with the Citizen's Military Training Camp and was able to compare himself with the abilities of the other officers. [1] Starting in 1933, at the age of

---

[1] The Citizens Military Training Camp was a program started by the government in 1920 with the intent to provide another source for the commissioning of officers for the army. Male citizens could obtain basic military training without an obligation to serve. Training was for one month each summer for four summers and could lead to commissioning as a 2nd Lt. in the army.

17 , while in high school Neil had spent 30 days each summer with the CMTC. In addition to ROTC summer camp he also participated in National Guard training from 1937 – 1940.

Butch had diligently planned on a military career and would have been fine with that and his current active duty orders except life had just gotten complicated. In his own words from his personal papers, he wrote " For the first time in my life, I was in love and deeply in love at that. My orders were for Camp Wolters, only 89 miles from home and the one I love, but now it seemed like 8,900 miles and it seemed the end of everything."

Neil had been introduced to his future wife, Mary Rue Speer, by a fraternity brother and life long friend, Phillip Montgomery, who like Butch was pre-med. Grades proved to be Butch's obstacle to his pre-med plans. Butch spent his time at Camp Wolters training soldiers for combat duty from about Nov. 1941 – March 1943.

Butch married Mary Rue Speer, daughter of Robert Moreland Speer and Ethyl Rue Jelleff Speer on March 21, 1942 in Dallas, Texas. The bride's family moved south to Dallas from Pennsylvania in the 1920's. Her father was in the retail furniture business. Both the bride and groom attended Highland Park High School in Dallas. Their first child, Mary Rue was born Feb. 16 1943. They would eventually have 3 more children, a daughter Carol, a son Mike and a daughter Marjorie.

1942 Wedding Photo Harris C. Neil, Harris C. Neil Jr, Robert M. Speer, Mary Rue Speer Neil, Maude Miller Neil, Mary Ethyl Rue Speer

Lt. Neil was promoted to 1st Lt. after completing the Officer's Basic Training Course April 28, 1943 – August 1, 1943 at Fort Benning, Georgia. Completion of this course would lead to permanent assignment to a unit readying for combat. The course's emphasis was on leadership, tactics, coordination of fire and air support, weapons familiarization, and many other subjects. 1st Lt. Neil was as ready as he would ever be.

Chapter Two

Europe

The United States officially entered the war in December 1941 after the Japanese sneak attack on Pearl Harbor. Talk immediately began about an invasion of Europe since the Axis (enemy) forces now occupied most of Europe. The U.S. was not prepared for war, but quickly mobilized both the military and industry to produce an efficient war machine. By the spring of 1944, the Allied forces had pushed the Axis forces out of North Africa and Italy. Russia was pressing Germany from the east. It was time to take the next step and invade Western Europe.

Lt. Neil crossed the Atlantic Ocean aboard the 8100-ton transport SS Susan B. Anthony. Top speed was 18 knots and Butch described the crossing as "very fine and uneventful". Dr. William McConahey described his trip on the same route as uneventful also. He said it was a boring trip with little to do. They wore their life preservers at all times. Abandon ship drills and anti- aircraft practice broke the monotony while money changed hands rapidly in dice and card games going on throughout the ship. The passage took about twelve days. A British band playing The Stars and Stripes Forever greeted McConahey's ship[2] Butch traveled up the Firth of Clyde and

---

[2] McConahey p14

arrived in Glasgow Scotland on May 23, 1944.

The Susan B. Anthony would later serve as a transport carrying many 90th Division (Butch's future Division) troops towards the Normandy beaches during the invasion. Unfortunately, she later hit a mine on June 7, 1944 and sank in the English Channel. All 2,689 persons aboard were saved.

At Glasgow, they remained on board the ship before debarking to the beauty of the Scottish springtime. Two miles away, they boarded what Butch described as tiny toy like railroad coaches and enjoyed the trip through the countryside. Our non-swimmer relished being on firm land after all those days at sea. Ten hours later, they arrived at a small wayside station and were trucked on the left side of the road (the English way) to Camp del a Mee, an old British army camp where they jammed into cold masonry buildings.

They bedded down in 65" x 30" bunks with burlap sacks filled with hay for mattresses. Little did they know that soon they would long for the luxury of those burlap sacks. The quarters were heated by small stoves, which were supplied with inadequate fuel, which they soon "supplemented" from the kitchen supply when no one was looking. His Company was classified as an excess Officers Company so they had no duty for four days and just relaxed until they were assigned duties like censor work and as training officers. While at Camp del a Mee, news was received about the June 6,1944 D-Day invasion via radio and newspapers. Dispatches were rosy and wagering was heavy that they would never get across the channel before the war was over.

Chapter Three

D-Day

Allied troops (160,000) under the command of the Allied Supreme Commander, Dwight Eisenhower landed on over sixty miles of the Normandy coast on D-Day. About half were American. The rest were British, Canadians and other nations. The Americans landed at Utah and Omaha Beach. The British and Canadians landed at Gold Juno and Sword Beach. The beaches above are listed from west to east.

On the night before, paratroopers were dropped behind enemy lines. The objective was to link landed troops with the paratroopers. The British and Canadians quickly gained their objectives and advanced 4 -5 miles. At Omaha, the Americans ran into grave danger and were still just clinging to the beach at sunset. Most of the amphibious tanks at Omaha had floundered and sunk approaching the beach and the infantry had little support here. One regiment of the 90th, the 359th landed on D-Day at Utah Beach. There was less resistance at Utah beach and the troops had amphibious tank support.

In addition, because of confusion, the Utah landings were actually made in the wrong location more than a mile south of the intended location.[3] The original planned location was more strongly defended and would have been in the range of enemy artillery, but the new location was not and this helped in the success of the attack.

Hobert Winebrunner a young infantryman in the 359th described his introduction to France:

"When that door went down, we scrambled out in a hurry. No one knew what to expect and we weren't about to take any chances. Getting off that beach topped everyone's list of objectives. We ran as fast as drenched clothes and over-sized field packs would allow. Only blurred boot prints remained in our sandy wake. "[4]

The Americans proceeded to fight inland through the green, thick, hedgerows of Normandy. The troops at Utah beach where the 90th Division went in managed to link up with airborne forces of the 82nd and 101st Airborne near Ste-Mere-Eglise. Butch's future 1st battalion secured a bloody bridge over the Merderet River at Chef-du-Pont and then took the town of Picauville by mid-morning. Pushing on towards Pont-l'Abbe they met fierce enemy resistance and had to dig in. The Germans stubbornly defended the ¾ of a mile from Picauville to Pont-l'Abbe . Fighting was from hedgerow to hedgerow.

---

[3] Ryan, p 232
[4] Winebrenner p.19-20

Chapter Four

Replacements

Lt. Neil and the other men back at Camp del a Mee were organized into company like unit packages of about 200 men and 8 officers. The men were trained, drilled and tested in these units. Lt. Neil traveled 30 miles to another camp and was placed in charge of package X-24-D consisting of 270 men and 15 officers. They moved out two days later on a train to a camp further south in England where they attended lectures, fired their weapons and trained.

All news from Normandy was still positive and it sounded like the Germans were getting drummed. At this time as part of the orientation, the officers were shown a large map showing where the allied lines were. Lt. Neil related that he looked at the map and " I felt quite weak." Our troops were barely on the coast. To look at the map, things looked quite bleak., but to listen and read about it, it seemed that all was going quite well. " Butch knew his package number X-24-D meant they would cross over 24 days after D-Day. He received secret orders for an ammunition allowance to be picked up at the next staging area. This looked like the real deal to him. They moved to a staging area and were ready to go, but they still did not leave and had no duties, so Butch proceeded to procure beer and let the men have a party. During the party, Butch received the orders that they were to go the next morning. After final inspection, they trucked to the train, loaded and moved further south where they trucked to Southhampton and straight to the waterfront. They were to board a ship within the next hour. Lt. Neil inquired about the ammunition they were to be issued, and was told there was none available. They would have to cross without it. Adding to the snafu, while he was turning over rosters to the port commander, the truck driver drove off with his carbine. With no weapon and no ammunition, the non-swimmer was not feeling very optimistic. " At this moment I didn't have too much desire for the nice boat ride we were going to take. " [5] After eating a cold K-ration, they finally boarded a British channel ship and departed 45 minutes later towards France and events that would either end or change their lives forever. The British transport carrying Butch sailed out of the harbor, anchored, waited until dark and joined a convoy of other ships for the passage. The British officers graciously opened their bar and state rooms to the American officers and Butch noted that it was a pleasant night for the officers although conditions were uncomfortable for the enlisted men who unlike the officers were crammed into the ship. Early the next morning as the sun welcomed a new day, the coast of France was quite visible. The ship dropped anchor around noon at the Omaha beach anchorage. They loaded into L.C.I. 's about three in the afternoon and all shuttled to shore. [6]

---

[5] Notes left in personal papers of H.C. Neil
[6] Notes left in personal papers of H.C. Neil

Chapter Five

90th Division

View from Inside of a German Pill Box, Utah Beach

Butch's future regiment, the 358th regiment of the 90th Division landed on Utah Beach on D-Day+2, June 8, 1944 in the VII Corps area. Utah beach is an expansive sandy beach that extends as far as the eye can see.

During the remainder of June , the 90th Division drove the enemy back through Pont l'Abbe, Gourbesville and Port-bail. Their progress was slow and resistance was stiff. The Germans had trained to fight in the Normandy hedgerows. The Americans had not even been told about them.

These hedgerows dating back to Roman times are mounds of earth enclosing a field to keep in cattle with only one opening into the field. Vegetation is grown on the mound and the roads running alongside feel sunken. Each field became a separate small battlefield fortification. The Germans developed tactics for defending these hedgerow battlefields. The Americans had to learn on the job with high casualties. By the middle of June, the Division had been chewed up and morale was low.[7]

From June 21st to about July 1st the Division had a front line of about 35KM (21.7 miles). The 357th was at Port-bail, extending east, the 359th was in the middle , and the 358th was on the left with the left flank at Baupte and Appeville. By late June, 1944, the port city of Cherbourg and the Corentin Peninsula were secured. Foret de Mont Castre and the bloody hill 122 was cleared on July 11, 1944 breaking the Mahlman Line, one of the enemy's toughest defensive positions. The capture of Hill 122 was a milestone for Lt. Neil's future 358th Infantry regiment. Casualties were extremely high. Only three officers of the 3rd battalion were not killed or wounded in the battle.[8] The 3rd battalion of the 358th regiment was awarded a Presidential Unit Citation for its key role in the defeat of the Germans.[9]

---

[7] Colby p 85
[8] Colby p117
[9] Colby p 118

Chapter Six

358th Regiment

Twenty-eight year old, Lt. H.C. Neil Jr. arrived in Normandy on July 1, 1944 as executive officer of replacement packet X-24- D.. He had been preparing for this since High School. At Southern Methodist University, he lettered on the fencing team and was a member of Phi Delta Theta where Harris "Butch" Neil kept three boa constrictors in the fraternity house to the consternation of the housemother. He would be asked to tame a more dangerous creature now. There were very high casualties in early July with a lot of confusion about unit strengths and personnel assignments that led to sudden changes in duty assignments. Lt. Neil was immediately assigned to the 90th Division. Initially, he was sent to K Co., 3rd Bn on July 15 as executive officer and transferred to Co. A on July 23.[10] In Butch's words, " After the attack on the Island where the 1st Bn was routed and lost a lot of men, including the Bn CO. I was sent to A Co, 1st Bn to take over as Commanding Officer. The officer, Lt. Baird, who was the Commanding Officer before the attack, showed up from somewhere and was given the company again. I was made Executive Officer, but

---

[10] Morning Report 20 July, 1944

it was decided I was needed more as a platoon leader, and I was given the 1st platoon."[11] What led to Lt. Neil's assignment was the following costly battle: On July 22,1944, a battle took place referred to as the Battle of the Island on the Seves River, northeast of Periers, where two battalions of the 90th , consisting primarily of green replacements with poor leadership, were routed by the Germans after attempting a suicidal daylight attack across open fields controlled by accurate German artillery. The battle of the island of Seves was the last major encounter for the 358th Infantry in the Normandy hedgerow country. It was the last German success in Normandy. Over 200 Americans were taken prisoner, 100 killed, and 500 wounded. This was a low point for the 90th. The 90th needed replacements more than any other division. It was losing men because of poor leadership. Leadership shakeups took place and Brigadier Raymond S. McClain, a distinguished Oklahoma City banker and exceptional officer took over the 90th. Under his command, the 90th would become one of the best divisions. [12] Lt. Neil assumed command of the 358th Regiment ,1st Bn, A Company, 1st platoon where he would remain .Tenure of an infantry lieutenant was 2 ½ weeks on average in the first seven weeks in Normandy.They were usually dead before they could learn the ropes. By January1945, the Americans had learned to utilize the night infiltration attack over daylight assaults and casualties were ¼ as much.

---

[11] letter dated 3 Dec. 1992 H.C. Neil to Vitus Bell
[12] Bradley p 269

Lt. H.C.Neil Jr. (Butch) in Normandy

The 358th moved rapidly to the south in the vicinity of St. Lo & Periers. The Germans were backing up to avoid being trapped and mining everything along the way. By July 29th, the 90th Division was in Monthuchon just north of Coutances.

The German mining decreased as their withdrawal speeded up .Opposition became sporadic. On July 30th, American armored units advanced rapidly out of the hedgerows now moving up to 24 miles a day. On July 31, General Patton was placed in charge of the armored units and they were in Avranches that day. Shortly thereafter, Patton was placed in charge of the entire 3rd army (which included the 90th). He sent two corps, including the 90th out east and south. The 90th was given the job of taking Ste-Hilaire-du-Harcouet, a town on the Selune River southeast of Avranches. The Division was divided into two task forces. The 358th regiment was in "Task Force Clarke" under the command of Lt. Col. Christian Clarke Jr. Task Force Clarke advanced easily, captured the bridge they needed and eliminated the light resistance in the town. Butch's 1st battalion had seized the high ground east of the town, 3rd battalion seized the bridge and 2nd battalion occupied the town. There were very few casualties. The liberated town celebrated the Americans with flowers and wine, but the Americans were advancing too rapidly to enjoy the hospitality.

Mayenne Bridge

The 90th was sent to take the City of Mayenne, a crossing point of six roads. They were to secure bridgeheads across the Mayenne River. Task force Weaver under the command of Brig. General William G. Weaver led the advance on Mayenne. They forced their way to the west bank of the Mayenne River by Aug, 5th.

It is recorded in Peragimus , "We Accomplish", a history of the 358th, that many of the Americans enjoyed a cool dip in the Mayenne River to escape the August heat. We know Lt. Butch did not participate in the swim.

"I don't believe we ever hit anything you couldn't do. I will make one exception and that is swim, and thank the good man above we never had to. "

letter from Carl Weingartner to Lt. H.C. Neil, 9 Dec. 1945

From Mayenne, the Americans moved quickly to capture Le Mans and overcame stiff resistance to capture this large city.

Chapter Seven

Le Mans

On the 2nd day of August, 1944 , 1st Battalion of the 358th moved from east of Ste Hilaire , then across the Mayenne River . A three-day march took them to Ste Suzanne. They were trucked to Le Mans three days later. The first battalion and second battalion moved to the northeast of the city. Second battalion crossed the Sarthe River northeast of Le Mans and the city was completely surrounded by the 90th Division. At this moment in the war the 90th Division was further into France than any other Allied unit . [13] They now were nicknamed the "Tough 'Ombres". Butch's A company, manning a roadblock northwest of the city at St. Suzanne, was among the furthest elements of the 90th into France. On 8, August 1944, the platoon's lookout anxiously reported to Butch that an enemy convoy was approaching their roadblock. Butch organized the men placing them on either side of the road for the ambush. Visibility was limited due to fog and Butch really did not know the strength of the enemy. He strolled out and halted the enemy column, and in the style of what was described as Jesse James, demanded the surrender of the amazed enemy while pointing to either side of the road. The shocked Germans looked around and immediately surrendered. Lt. Neil's platoon had captured two large enemy motorized columns with over 150 prisoners. [14]

---

[13] Peragimus, "We Accomplish"

[14] The "outlaw" Butch Neil was awarded a silver star for this action. (Jan. 15th,1945 citation award of oak leaf cluster to silver star)

Chapter Eight

Falaise

About Aug. 15, the 90th was ordered to be part of the mission to reduce the Falaise pocket and cut off the retreating German Army Group B that was retreating north towards Germany. The mission of the 90th was to attack north , seize the village of Ommeel and the high ground west of Chambois. The main German Seventh Army escape route ran directly through Chambois making control of the town vital to the Americans and the Germans. [15] The Battle of the Falaise Pocket, or Falaise Gap, fought from 12–21 August 1944, was the decisive engagement of the battle of Normandy. The name came from the pocket around the town of Falaise within which Army Group B consisting of the German Seventh and Fifth Panzer Armies became encircled by the advancing Allied forces. The Germans desperately sought to maintain an escape gap or corridor to allow their retreat. This battle resulted in the destruction of the bulk of Germany's forces west of the Seine River and opened the way to the German border.

After the American breakout from the Normandy beachhead (Operation Cobra), rapid advances were made to the south and southeast by General Patton's Third Army. Facing both the U.S. penetration and

---

[15] Colby p 215

simultaneous British and Canadian offensive forces moving off their D-Day beachheads south of Caen, the Germans were ordered by Hitler to hold and counterattack. They lacked the resources and the German position was becoming more precarious day by day. Withdrawal to fight another day was the strategic move despite orders from Hitler to stand.

Seizing the opportunity to surround the entire German force, on 8 August, the Allied ground forces commander, General Montgomery ordered his armies to converge on the Falaise-Chambois area. The U.S. First Army formed the southern arm, the British Second Army the base, and the Canadian First Army the northern arm of the encirclement. The Germans fought hard to keep an escape route open. Their withdrawal began 17 August. On 19 August, the Allies linked up in Chambois ,but were too weak to completely seal the pocket. Gaps were forced in the Allied lines by desperate German assaults. The most significant and hard-fought gap was a corridor running past elements of the Polish 1st Armored Division, who had established a commanding position in the mouth of the pocket. The pocket was closed on August 21 with around 50,000 Germans trapped inside. Although it is estimated that significant numbers managed to escape, German losses in both men and material were massive. It was a fatal mistake by the Germans to not immediately withdraw as the Allies attempted to envelop them. The Allies had achieved a decisive victory. Paris was liberated on August 23 and by August 30th, the last German remnants had retreated across the Seine .

During Falaise, the 80th and 90th Divisions were sent north from Le Mans toward Alencon. They took Beaumont and Carrouges blasting through the enemy with armor with the infantry mopping up the German pockets left behind. On August 11, a French armored task force captured the undefended Sarthe River bridges at Alencon. On August 12, the Germans sent the 116th Panzer Division to Argentan to hold off the Americans and French. French and American armored divisions claimed almost 100 tanks destroyed and nearly 1500 prisoners.

Butch's 358th regiment was involved in house to house fighting in Argentan. About this time, Patton was ordered to halt his advance. Allied command feared that the Americans and Canadians merging together would cause too many friendly fire casualties. It was a mistake and instead of wiping out the entire German army, many were allowed to escape to defensive positions in Germany.

By August 16th, the Germans were fighting and running for their lives through a 15-mile gap. American artillery and tanks opened up on the fleeing Germans and it was a slaughter. From Major Bill Falvey's journal , we note that on Aug. 18th, Butch's 1st battalion of the 358th moved on Ste- Eugenie and Bon -Menil and took them by evening.

" Now as the trap was becoming closed it was like a large funnel which was about 40 miles high by about 16 miles wide at the bottom. There were many troops holding the sides of the funnel, but the 90th Division was alone at the bottom end of it, and German troops were pouring through the bottom like water over a dam." [16] " On August 19th, the 1st battalion of the 358th held the line from Ste -Eugenie to Bon -Menil and during the fighting two Pfcs., Caldwell and Geibelstein, knocked out four German tanks with five bazooka rounds. Both received the DSC. [17]

Carnage at Falaise gap from Lt. Neil's position

[16] Colby p223
[17] Colby p225

About the middle of the day on August 20th, the jaws of the Allied trap were completely closed by the 3rd battalion of the 358th when they closed the roads north and east of Chambois. Outnumbered by the stream of Germans, the 3rd battalion of the 358th stood it's ground during the fierce battle. "Anyone and everyone not hauling ammo or feeding a machine gun, fired something. Our weapons rattled on by the hour, without remission. My hands and fingers were so twisted and cramped. My arms ached. Yet we dared not rest. There were targets to spare, more by the minute."[18]

Major Falvey's journal relates that "At the end of the battle , the Germans were in a sort of a circle with a diameter of about 8 miles. They were being shelled and fired at from all sides. I went up in an airplane ride over the remains of the battlefield. It was estimated there were 8,000 dead German soldiers and hundreds of dead horses in the trap. There were knocked out tanks, self propelled guns, and artillery pieces everywhere one looked. The stench of death was so bad one could hardly stand it in an airplane." [19]

 Col. Hans Von Luck , a German Panzer Division commander, was located on the heights west of Vimoutiers where he had a wide view of the valley. "Enemy planes were swooping down uninterruptly on anything that moved. We could do nothing to help.

---

[18] Winebrenner p10
[19] Colby p241

A line from a poem about the Crusades in 1213 came to him: "Man , horse, and truck by the Lord were struck."[20] Col. Hans Von Luck estimated German Falaise Gap casualties at 10,000 men killed and 40,000 men captured, including several GHQs and remains of some 15 divisions , mainly infantry. 40,000 – 50,000 were able to escape.[21] The 90th Division suffered less than 600 casualties. [22]

---

[20] Von Luck p 205
[21] Von Luck p 206
[22] Winebrenner p116 (via Abrams p24)

Chapter Nine

Reims

The 90th was then reassigned to XX Corps and the Third Army. They stayed near Chambois for about three days resting and putting people and equipment back together. On August 25, the American Seventh Army and the French Army landed at Marseilles in southern France and started working their way north towards Germany. On Aug. 26th, the Yanks secured Fontainebleau and the Seine River crossing there. This was the closest that they would come to Paris as French forces were given the honor of liberating Paris. The next mission was the historic city of Reims. The 7th Armored Division spearheaded the attack towards Reims, with the 90th on its left and the 5th on its right. This drive carried the 90th through the famous battlefields of WWI to near Verdun. On August 26th, the 358th moved over 175 miles through Mamers, La Ferte -Bernard, Chateaudun, Pithiviers and Malesherbes. There was little resistance as the Germans had pulled back to the fortress of Metz. On the other side of Paris, the allies were also moving north. Strategically, the main drive on Germany was to take place on this side of Paris close to the coast from which resupply would be easy. The attack would thrust into the German Ruhr valley, the industrial heart of Germany. The advance to the south by Patton's third army towards Berlin would be secondary. The bulk of supplies and gasoline would go to the main drive.

On the 29th the 90th crossed the Marne River at Chateau -Thierry, a famous WWI battlefield about 30 miles from Paris, at a bridge being held by French forces. The 357th reg. seized and crossed two more river crossings , the LaVesle and the Aisne . They then moved through Reims on Sept. 1, covering the last 23 miles on foot. [23] They had liberated thousands of square miles at a rapid fuel-consuming pace. Butch's "A" company guarded the bridges of Reims while the rest of the Regiment carried out security missions to the east near Warmeriville. Due to a gasoline shortage, the advance halted and did not resume again until Sept. 5. The 1st battalion moved near Verdun on Sept.5. [24]

Butch's platoon guarding bridge in Reims

[23] Colby p245
[24] Peragimus, "We Accomplish"

Butch relates in correspondence after the war that regrettably he did not start a written journal until Sept. 1, 1944. The first diary entry describes "no moving". This is noteworthy to him because the last weeks had been a whirlwind of rapid movements.

Diary Entry (Lt. H.C. Neil)

1 Sept. *1944* : *Reims, France-Outposting bridge. 2nd day here- No new developments No moving.*

The next four days would be spent guarding a bridge across the Canel de l'Aisne a' la Marne in the beautiful city of Reims, a wonderful period to look back on in the tense days to come.

Chapter Ten

Mairy-Mainville

On Sept. 5, 1944 they traveled about 23 miles to St. Hilaire- le Grande. As they were foot soldiers, 13 miles were traveled by foot. The next day they trucked to Sedan passing through Verdun and picking up some noteworthy French bread on the way. On September 7, Butch relates that they trucked to Spincourt to meet an enemy group of 10 tanks and fifty men. The Germans had left and the men out posted at the railway station. Then they trucked to Mont-Bonvillers and walked a couple of miles to Mairy-Mainville where they set up defensive positions for the night.

About this time, the Division Command Post was moved to a position more forward than usual. The words of Maj. General , William G. Weaver , Asst. Div. CO explain why: "During this period it was decided to move the Division Command Post well forward to avoid the continual changing of location brought about by the fast advancing situation."[25]

---

[25] Colby p 256

During the night of September 7,1944, an enemy
surprise attack hit the Division command post near
Mont, and then turned towards Butch and the 1st
battalion in the town of Mairy- Mainville. Both the
Germans and Americans were surprised at the
command post incident. The newly equipped German
106 Panzer Brigade with factory fresh tanks made an
accidental attack on the command post. They were en-
route southward from Audun-le-Roman with the 19th
Volksgrenadier Division to reinforce their garrison at
Briey with the intention of attacking the 90th Infantry
Division. They split into two columns, the Stossgruppe
1 advancing via Mont-Bonvilliers and the Stossgruppe
2 via Trieux. The Germans unwisely did no forward
scouting. At 0200, the main column split near Murville
with half moving down the main route N43 and half
moving along a small country road towards the
villages of Mont and Mairy. The Germans stumbled
into the American Command Post, which was camped
in woods southeast of Landres. Roads ran on either
side of the campsite. Around 0200, at least half the
German column from Stossgruppe 1 passed the
American position before the foes recognized each
other. About 0300, an American tank fired at the
Germans destroying a German half-track. German
tanks then turned and fired destroying the US tank.
The Germans inflicted heavy casualties on the
Americans with many dying in their sleep. The
Command Post officers evacuated to the rear and
other American tanks from the 712th Tank Bn. went
into the fight, but they were reluctant to fire in the
dark because they knew friendly troops were all
around.

Stossgruppe 1 continued to move towards Briey. The tanks and support troops became spread out in the pre-dawn darkness as the Americans rallied. The Germans expected any Americans they hit with their tank forces to retreat as this is what they had experienced in Russia. Instead, the American infantry began to attack the Germans. In the light of daybreak, part of Stossgruppe 1 commenced an attack on Mairy that was occupied by Butch's 1st Battalion, 358th Infantry, supported by towed anti-tank guns from the 607th Tank Destroyer Battalion.

Mairy -Mainville is a peaceful red tile roofed village surrounded by hills . It sits in a depression and the steeple from the church dominates the village. Around 0700, German tanks opened up on Mairy from the high ground towards Mont. US anti-tank guns returned fire knocking out a couple of German tanks. At 0800, from the south side of Mairy along the Mainville road, 11 German SdKfz-25 armored half-tracks attacked the town. Two were blown apart at close range by the US infantry cannon company and their 105mm howitzers. Two more were destroyed by bazooka fire from the 1st Bn , 358 th. [26]Four more were eliminated by anti-tank guns as they fled to the north. Around 0850, a group of German tanks from the main column tried to sneak towards the village down a sunken farm road. Infantry led by Butch disabled the lead panther tank.

---

[26] Capt. Cud T. Baird III, was awarded a Distinguished Service Cross for knocking out these two tanks with a bazooka and leading a successful counterattack while wounded.

Wick Fowler, staff correspondent for the Dallas
Morning News reported the event in an article dated
Nov. 23, 1944 as follows:

Outnumbered more than they like to think about, a
Dallas infantry officer and twenty doughboys ripped
open a German armored column in a little village east
of Verdun, costing the enemy almost unbelievable
casualties without a loss of a man in their own little
band. Leader of the platoon of the 358th Infantry
regiment of the 90th Division was First Lt. Harris C.
Neil from Dallas. In the group were other Texans,
including PFC Edward Dowell, Brekenridge, PFC John
C. Strong, Henderson, 2nd Lt. William V. Kilpatrick,
Paris, and Sgt. Jose Pilon, Roma, down in the Rio
Grande Valley.

   "We set up a night defensive position in the town.
" Lt. Neil said. (Mairy) . "About daylight, I was
ordered to report to the company command post (at
Mont) ,a tiny crossroads about 3 miles due west) with
twenty men for a special mission. We started moving
toward the CP when a platoon runner came up and
said the enemy was attacking the town with tanks and
armored cars. I then saw the first vehicle. It was a tank.
It was knocked out by a tank destroyer. In the column
were six Mark VI tanks and thirty-three armored cars.
We forgot about our mission and went to work on
those Jerries. Enemy troops from the knocked out tank
were getting out and running for a potato patch. We
got behind a stonewall and fired on them. The Jerries
were firing back at us, but my boys just stood up and
let them have it. Apparently the Germans in that

column were more surprised than we were , and we supposed we had by-passed them when we moved into the town and that they were trying to make an escape."

Mairy- Mainville 1944 . German Carnage

"We kept up that firing for about fifteen minutes. Lt. Kilpatrick and three of his men from another platoon came up and he took two of my men and moved to a house so we could get into position to really assault the vehicles. With the rest of the men, I moved down a barbed wire fence to where we were just above the Germans. We got within twenty yards of them. Dowell fired a rifle grenade at the lead tank and when the Jerries piled out, we polished them off with rifles and machine guns. [27] He hit the second tank with a bazooka. The other vehicles poured 20mm fire at us. They couldn't get at us with their 88s.

Mairy -Mainville 2015

When the fighting died down, we had 200 German prisoners, had killed another 100 and we learned later that 123 wounded Germans passed through our medical clearing

---

[27] For this action ,Lt. Neil received a silver star. The citation documents that from a range of twenty yards, he swept the enemy column with the fire of a heavy machine gun held in his hands, heedless of enemy fire of all calibers . His coolness during the action inspired all who witnessed.

station. When the big fight started, Lieutenant Kilpatrick and his platoon were at a roadblock. The column cut about half of his men off for nearly an hour and it was necessary to turn our artillery into their position in order to free them. Sargent Pilon was one of the men in that hot spot. " That artillery sure was hot, he said. "I just hugged a ditch. Those Jerries were within four or five yards of me. " The First Battalion in this action knocked out seven tanks and blew more than forty-eight armored vehicles to kingdom come. Division wide the 90th had captured or destroyed 30 tanks,60 halftracks and an estimated 100 miscellaneous vehicles and captured 764 prisoners in the vicinity of Mairy. [28]

Eventually, the Germans lost the bulk of their vehicles and the remainder retreated desperately to the north. Only 17 German tanks and 9 armored vehicles made it back to German lines along with a small portion of their support troops. Tactics that had been successful on the Eastern front had failed against the Tough 'Ombres of the 90th whose own divisional history downplays the fact that they effectively had eliminated an entire German panzer brigade.

---

[28] Pergimus, "We Accomplish "

The next day describes an incident involving Lt. Neil wandering out by himself, probably for some peaceful self reflection. There would be no peace.

9 Sept. 1944 : *Left position at **Mairy** on foot and went to _____ then moved on to **Haute**. Set up by railroad track- Then later moved out by self to farmhouse. Cleaned it (about 600 yds. in front of Co. found 5 live Germans- 3 wounded + 2 dead.)Then moved to right to cross road which was across **Bogelier** in Germany- Set up outpost on hill about 400 yds. from cross road- No new developments-Spent very cold night.*

The dairy entry above is rather subtle in its message. I had to read it multiple times, before I realized that Lt. Neil had entered a farmhouse by himself where he found five "live" Germans. Upon exiting, he left behind two dead Germans and had three wounded prisoners. I am not sure he would be welcomed anytime soon by any Germans to do "cleaning."

Chapter Eleven

Thionville

10 Sept. 1944: *Moved out through very dense woods to town of Angevillers where we set up defenses for night – Was shelled – Spent night in this position- Cold*

The 1st battalion defensive position put them in place to attack the high ground northwest of Thionville. The Morning report for Sept. 11 puts Neil's unit near Elange on the high ground above Thionville

12 Sept. 1944 :*Moved out towards Thionville. Captured high hills around City . Set up positions on edge of town while it was shelled – Spent night in this position- cold*

The Germans fought a withdrawing action as they were pushed back to the Moselle River. Thionville, an industrial city on the banks of the Moselle, was contested house by house. The 2nd battalion pushed them out and they withdrew destroying the last bridge over the river as they went. Butch and the 1st battalion followed up the 2nd battalion and primarily mopped up the remaining Germans in the north half of the city.

13 Sept. 1944: Moved down into left side of City of Thionville- Searched out buildings – No resistance- In afternoon 1st platoon moved up to town of Manom to search it out and clear it. Met no resistance- Moved back to Thionville and out posted in positions along the river- Remained here throughout the night – Were shelled (heavy) during night

The next day found Butch back in position in the heights above Thionville. On Sept. 15, he was ordered to lead a patrol across the Moselle River near the railroad bridge in order to scout out the railroad yards. This patrol was called off at this time. The next day, the patrol was reduced to 10 men led by another Lieutenant after he lost a coin flip with Butch. Butch led a patrol of a dozen men that would provide covering machine gun fire for the crossing patrol. This patrol set off in a raft, but could not land because of heavy enemy fire. All communication was lost with the patrol. Six men eventually got back and they all returned to their base camp at 2:30 am.

They remained in place on the rainy 17 and 18th of Sept, finally moving to new positions on the riverbank on the afternoon of September 19. On the next day, they spotted two GI's stranded underneath the middle of the bridge near the water signaling for help. They could not return. Major Lytle distinguished himself that night with the daring rescue of the two survivors while under fire [29] They got them safely back returning at 4 a.m. Lytle would later command the battalion when they attacked Fort Koenigsmacker. Butch and his men remained in the same position through September 26. His diary notes that Blood & Guts (Patton) was in the area looking things over. Before the 90th Division began its attack across the Moselle , General Patton had visited all the divisions involved in the effort to take Metz. The 90th got a message that went something like this .

" I've been giving hell to everybody, but I don't need to chew out you bastards. I just stopped by to say hello, because I thought you would be insulted if I didn't. You bastards sure know how to fight ! You always do more than I ask you to , and I ask plenty! [30]

---

[29] Lytle was awarded the Distinguished Service Cross for this feat
[30] McConahey p 93

The 27th of September brought an early morning 12-mile move by truck to Auvil and then on to Ste Marie - aux -Chenes where they went into defensive positions. Their command post was quartered in a schoolhouse.

The next day Butch attended a "battalion" meeting to be briefed on the big picture on the fronts. The big picture at the end of the third week of September was that Allied offensive operations were experiencing the pinch of an unfavorable logistical situation. The fight for the Arnhem bridgehead in Holland was going against the Allies. The First Army was attempting to drive to crack the West Wall at Aachen and the Third Army was attempting to expand a bridgehead east of the Moselle. Shortage of supplies threatened to limit all of these operations.

General Eisenhower announced that the focus would be on securing the port of Antwerp to provide another deep-water port. Priority would be given to the Allied effort to secure this port. Therefore, priority for supplies would go towards this effort rather than Third Army's push through the Metz and Moselle areas. General Patton was not happy with this restraint being put on the Third Army. Patton was authorized by his superior General Bradley to take limited actions as opportunities presented themselves. He was authorized to make minor adjustments to his lines so he made plans for continuing his attacks despite meager supplies. Patton wanted to drive a wedge into the concentric ring of Metz fortifications. Fort Driant was one that had been marked as very important.

Chapter Twelve

Metz

Lt. Neil would have learned about the current stalemate in the region and the battle for Ft. Driant to the south that had started the day before and ended in disaster for the American 5th infantry Division. Fort Driant was located five miles southwest of Metz, just west of the Moselle River. Originally constructed in 1902, the fort was constantly being beefed up throughout World War II by both the French and German armies. Fort Driant was made from steel reinforced concrete and was surrounded by a deep 60' wide dry moat and blanketed with treacherous barbed wire. It housed four main gun batteries of 100mm or 150mm guns, trenches, armored machine gun and observation posts. From its dominating position on the top of a hill 360 meters in height, it could direct heavy fire throughout the Moselle River Valley .

The Germans intended to make the most of the ring of forts around Metz, the ancient gateway city through which so many invading armies had passed. Metz was to be the linchpin in the Germans' defensive strategy. No army had directly taken the city since 1552. It had been captured after a 54-day siege during the Franco Prussian War and had been improved by the Germans during WWI although many of the fortifications in the area were in ruins.

Hitler had ordered a strategy of hold at all costs for fixed positions. Withdrawals were not allowed.

When the U.S. Third army arrived at Metz, they were stalemated by the German defenders for weeks over control of the city and its perimeter. Upon sustaining heavy losses attacking the fortifications, it was clear to the Americans that Fort Driant would have to be taken . Patton ordered the 5th Infantry Division to take Fort Driant.

No adequate maps existed for the Americans to guide the troops until after the initial assaults. The American army had advanced so fast that planners had made no provision for decent maps at this date. The Army was using mostly 1 :100,000 Michelin road maps that were inadequate for the type of information needed. No one had any idea of the actual design of the forts. The forts were so well camouflaged by vegetation that aerial photographs were of little help. [31] On the morning of September 27, 1944 ,P-47's from the XIX Tactical Air Command began bombing Fort Driant with 1,000 pound bombs and napalm. E Company, G Company and the 818th Tank Destroyer Company followed with their attack on Fort Driant. Small arms fire, machine guns, and mortars met the advancing troops. Most of the fort was below ground, causing the tank destroyers to be ineffective against the armored pillboxes.

---

[31] Kemp p 42

The initial attack faltered and the Americans withdrew to their original position in the afternoon. The attack resumed at noon on October 3 with bulldozers that attempted to fill in the fort's trench line and to place snakes, that were long pipes filled with explosives. The bulldozers and snakes proved to be of little help because during the second wave the bulldozers experienced mechanical difficulties and the snakes were either bent or lost. Upon reaching the perimeter, the German defenders were ready. Hand-to-hand fighting with grenades and gunfire broke out between the two sides. E Company managed to capture the southernmost barracks. An underground passage was located. The passage was heavily defended by machine guns and sniper fire, making exploitation of the tunnel impossible. The Germans lost roughly a quarter of the fort before the Americans withdrew on October 12-13, losing 64 killed, 547 wounded and 187 missing in action. A further attack on Fort Driant was deemed too costly.

The higher-ranking American officers involved in this operation were reluctant to bring it to an unsuccessful conclusion. It represented the first publicized reverse suffered by the Third Army. Much had been learned that would be put into training troops to attack fortified positions during October. Air power had proved to be of little help against a fortified position. These lessons would be put into play during November by Butch's platoon at Fort Koenigsmacker resulting in the reduction of the Metz fort system. [32]

---

[32] Cole p 275

By October 9, Patton had decided to bypass Driant. The men of the 5th Infantry Division were thought to be becoming battle fatigued and other operations were taking place around Metz with much greater success. When Metz fell in December 1944, Fort Driant finally surrendered to the 5th Infantry Division at 3:45 pm on December 8.

Chapter Thirteen

October Lull

During the October lull, General Walker instituted a period of training and rest. Units were pulled out of the front line by rotation and sent to rest camps in the rear. Personal gear and letters from home had caught up with the men for the first time since Normandy. There were hot baths and meals. More importantly, a serious training program taught the men how to attack fortified positions.. There was a determination to not be involved in another Fort Driant type disaster.[33]

Butch's diary entries for Sept. 29 – Oct. 8, describe a lot of training and down time. He notes the men were trained with bazookas, standard grenades, white phosphorous grenades and the use of demolition explosives against fortified positions. Polls for voting were open on Oct. 6 and Butch gathered and turned in the ballots on Oct. 14. Worthy of entry in his brief diary was the Red Cross Club mobile where they were given coffee and doughnuts.

---

[33] Kemp p 128

The army had learned that it was wise to give troops down time, but at this time there were no big rest areas in the Metz area. Rest for most guys consisted of a few hours behind the lines in some village where they might find a hot shower, coffee and doughnuts served by the Red Cross in a Red Cross "Club mobile". Some got to see movies or "jeep shows" performed by soldier performers. Radio broadcasts by the Armed Forces Network or music broadcasts from Berlin provided prime entertainment. The daily newspaper, *Stars and Stripes* and weekly Yank arrived with rations, cigarettes and morale boosting mail from home.

October 9th was spent with more demolitions training and training with flamethrowers. Lt. Neil improved the dugout where he was living the next day. He noted that the ground was rocky and hard so they "had to use T.N.T. to break through." Butch was not going to let that army explosives training go to waste ! Of course by the time they had really improved the living quarters, they got orders to move out about 4 miles to new woods to relieve cavalry positions .

October 17 - 22 diary entries indicated that they are pretty much in the same positions most of the time. Lt. Neil must have been getting restless because the next diary entry reads as follows:

23 Oct. 1944 : Still in the same area with the same mission. Ordered champagne for "break period"- No new developments- Rain during the night- Cold & Muddy-

October 24- 26 diary entries note an early morning move to Gravelotte and on to Rezonville and then to Mars-la-Tour where they took up new defensive positions. Butch and his men received some new clothing and shoes. They moved out the next day taking a position in a barn near Vauville. On Oct. 28th, they did bazooka and small arms firing training. They were shelled that night and one round hit the command post , but resulted in no casualties. Early the next morning, they moved to a rest area near St. Marie where they had dinner and went to a dance . They departed the rest area on October 31st and spent Halloween back in defensive positions in a barn near Verneville,

Chapter Fourteen

End of the Lull

The Regimental History , 358th Battalion summarizes
November 1944 :

" .....the month of November was to embrace one of the
most memorable periods in the history of the 358th
Infantry regiment and occupy a prominent place in the
annals of American Military operations."

*1 Nov. 1944 : Moved out at 0800 on trucks to Bivouac Area
in old French Garrison near_____ (at*
Montfontaine, France per AIOC 1947 -1948) *Arriving
here at 1100. Set up in two houses. Spent afternoon getting
set up &   cleaned up- No new developments- Cold-Clear*

*2 Nov.1944 : In the same location with same set up-
Training schedule started with exercises this morning &
group games this afternoon, No new developments- Cold-
Clear*

One part of the training consisted of dry run river crossings. They practiced boat loading and paddling of the M2 assault boat. The M2 assault boat was a 13' 5 " long x 5'-11" wide x 2'-1" high plywood, seat-less scow style boat . It had a squared bow, a flat vertical stern and a fairly flat bottom. Displacement was 4,000 pounds and it could carry 15 men, three of which were to be engineers assigned to the boat. There were handrails on the sides to help in transport of the boat to the water. Fully loaded the boat cleared the water by only 8" so it was not designed for rough water. Two boats could be secured end to end so the boat could even function as a bridge pontoon.

M2 Assault Boat (U.S. Army Signal Corps)

The next days saw no advancement, but rather consisted of training ,preparation and rest.

7 Nov. 1944 :Received orders to prepare to move out- Are to move out by truck at 1600. Moved out to_____ , Had supper there, went by truck to

_____ dismounted, walked 5 miles to assembly area in woods- Arrived about 4:00 on 8 Nov.

Officers were then issued aerial photos, and detailed engineering maps of Ft. Koenigsmacker

On November 7, in an operation cloaked by a complicated deception scheme known as operation Casanova, the 90th , traveling without lights or unit makings was moved into their assembly area in the forest of Cattenom that was directly opposite the crossing site. The deception operation was successful because the 90th did achieve surprise.[34]

---

[34] Kemp p147

General Eisenhower and the army planners had committed to pushing on across a broad front with winter approaching. The plan in the area of Metz, France was to surround the city and choke it off. The XX Corps with the 90th Division would circle the city from the north while the XII Corps would come in from the south. The flooding Moselle River had to be bridged because the Germans had destroyed the existing bridges. Then armored units could cross and prevent German reinforcement and resupply. After that, the Americans could advance on the Rhine River.

 The 358th regiment would advance to the small town of Cattenom, along the west bank of the Moselle.. This area was strategic because construction of a bridge was feasible here unlike most of the river. Across the river was the German Ft. Koenigsmacker, part of the Maginot Line. Ft. Koenigsmacker was a key fortified position dominating all approaches to the Moselle River, which the 90th Division needed to cross in order to complete, the encirclement of German held city fort of Metz, France.

The objective for the 358th Regiment was to take the fort in a frontal infantry assault. The 359th Regiment would swing to the north of the fort to Malling and the 357th to the south of the fort.

Chapter Fifteen

Ft. Koenigsmacker

Just to the southeast of Basse- Ham, France, the ground rises to form the heights upon which Fort Koenigsmacker is located. From this high spot, the entire flat area extending over to the Cattenom Forest could be viewed. There was a six-mile view all the way to Thionville to the south. The view to the north extended to Metrich.   Dr. William McConahey, Battalion Surgeon for the 357th regiment describes Ft. Koenigsmacker as "the key to the enemy defenses in this area, one of the most formidable forts I've ever seen. It was a series of steel and concrete strongpoints built into the top of a commanding hill, and so well concealed that little could be seen of it above ground. Underground passages, dozens of machine –gun emplacements, anti –tank ditches, four disappearing artillery pieces and so forth made it an extremely strong fort. "[35]

 Fort Koenigsmacker (coordinates 49.37982N 6.25778E) was built 1908 -1914 after the annexation of the Moselle by the Germans following the Franco-Prussian war. It was part of the Maginot group of forts designed to thwart future French attempts to regain the Alsace and Lorraine areas.

---

[35] McConahey p. 95

1944, Ft. Koenigsmacker ,Shelter Point 4

Along with Metrich Fort , 4,000 yards to the northeast and Fort d' Illange , 3 miles to the southwest, the three forts completely commanded the Moselle basin and the highways extending along either side of the river. Each fort's artillery tied in with that of the other.

 Ft. Koenigsmacker lies on a high area that rises from the village of Basse -Ham at about 150 meters to 210 meters over a distance of 500 meters. (a 197 ft. rise in 1640 feet.... or to illustrate imagine climbing up a 10 story building on a ramp 5 ½ American football fields long).

In World War I, the fort saw no action because it was located behind the lines of combat. Koenigsmacker's innovative design was a roughly pentagonal shape consisting of four dispersed fortified barracks built into a hillside .The tops of the fortified barracks were protected by 6- 8 feet of concrete and surrounded by parapets. The barrack rears were built underground and thus shielded by earth. The fort mounted four 100 mm long guns at its top in completely revolving turrets of 3 -4 " thick steel. They had been removed from the German fortifications of Metz and had an artillery range of 7.9 miles. Deep networks of barbed wire surrounded all of this. Perimeter blockhouses linked by the fort's tunnel system had lines of fire across the barbed wire that completely overlapped. Corridors inside the pillboxes led to a staircase that led to basement floors in the underground corridors of the main fort.

At the top of the main concrete fort structure was a series of cupola like armored observation posts. They had narrow slits, which permitted safe observation. Direct hits from artillery had no effect on them. All approaches to the steel doors of the fort were blocked by an 8'-0" high spiked fence which was covered by machine gun emplacements. Trenches in the interior of the position were for infantry. There were 8 one story concrete pillboxes built in the intervals connecting via underground tunnels totaling 8,500 feet in length. A diesel powered central utility plant generated electricity that provided the comfort of central heat for the barracks.

The 74th infantry regiment, 19th Volksgrenadier Division, manned the fort under the command of (Colonel Karl Britzelmayr) of the LXXXII Corps of the German First Army. In early November, there were no German tanks in the area. However there were 40 – 50 anti-tank guns. The Germans were depending on the fortifications, natural terrain, massive minefields (40,000 mines) and the river obstacle to deter the Americans. It almost did.

Chapter Sixteen

A Simple Plan

Basic strategy during an attack called for a division to commit two regiments to action with a third regiment held in reserve. Each regiment would usually commit two battalions in action with the third held for reserve support. At battalion level, two companies would be committed to the assault with a third in reserve. There was usually a fourth heavy weapons company in reserve also. At the platoon level , the same pattern held with two rifle platoons attacking with another platoon in direct support.

Each rifleman was armed with an M1 semi-automatic (Garand) rifle that fired eight rounds per clip or an M1 carbine that fired 17 rounds per clip. The range of the M1 rifle was 500-1,000 yards and the M1 carbine had an effective range of 300 yards. Most men preferred the rifle.

The army tactical plan for crossing a major river was simple. You meet in assembly areas to complete preparations, move into attack positions close to the river, load twelve men and three engineers to a boat, and cross the river in assault boats under the cover of darkness . Then the engineers would bring the boats back after crossing in order to bring across successive waves. Once landed across the river, you captured the area around the landing site. When the areas were secure, the engineers would build bridges to allow more troops and equipment to cross.[36] It looked easy on paper.

First Battalion of the 358th was to cross on the right at the village of Basse -Ham across from Ft. Koenigsmacker and take that fort by storm. Third Battalion was to cross opposite the town that shared the name of Koenigsmacker with the fort and take it. Second Battalion was to remain in reserve and then relieve Third Battalion. Lt. Col. C.A Lytle , Battalion commander ordered the First Battalion across in four waves. In addition, the village of Basse -Ham was to be taken so that the flank could be protected. An aid station was to be set up across the river here also. The decision to put the aid station across the river saved many lives.

2014, Fort Koenigsmacker Shelter Point 4

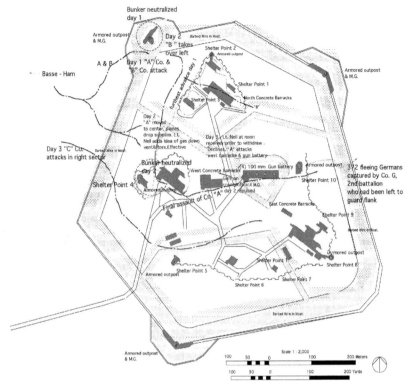

Bunker neutralized
day 1

Armored outpost
& M.G.

Day 2
"B " takes
over left

Barbed Wire in Moat

Shelter Point 2

Armored outpost

A & B

Day 1 "A" Co. &
"B" Co. attack

Basse - Ham

Armored outpost
& M.G.

Shelter Point 1

furthest advance day 1

Shelter Point 3

North Concrete Barracks

Day 2
"A" moves
to center, planes
drop supplies. Lt.
Neil adds idea of gas down
ventilators. Effective

Day 3 , Lt. Neil at noon
receives order to withdraw .
Declines. "A" attacks
west barracks & gun battery

Day 3 "C" Co.
attacks in right sector

Barbed Wire in Moat

Bunker neutralized
day 2

West Concrete Barracks

(4) 100 mm Gun battery

Armored outpost

372 fleeing Germans
captured by Co. G,
2nd battalion
who had been left to
guard flank

Shelter Point 4

Armored outpost

German
counterattack M.G.
"A" day 2 repulsed

Shelter Point 10

Final assault of Co. "A"

East Concrete Barracks

Shelter Point 9

Barbed Wire in Moat.

Shelter Point 11

Armored outpost

Shelter Point 5

Shelter Point 8

Armored outpost

Shelter Point 6

Shelter Point 7

Barbed Wire in Moat

Armored outpost
& M.G.

Scale 1 : 2,000

100   50   0   100   200 Meters

100   50   0   100   200 Yards

FORT KOENIGSMACKER

© 2014 chris johnston architect

72

Chapter Seventeen

Ft. Koenigsmacker,Diary

Days of continuous rain preceded the American attack.
Dirt roads were just soupy mud. The night of 9
November was pitch black.

*8 Nov 1944.: Rain- Cold- Got briefed on our attack +
crossing of Moselle river. Spent day getting ready and
making plans. Were to move out at 0100 9 Nov-Cold rain*

*9 Nov. 1944 :Moved out at 0100 to town nearby-picked up
boats and marched to river-Crossed without enemy fire-
Advanced up and got into positions on our objective-
Strongpoint #4   took positions – top of the fort, then spent
day trying to secure inside of fort-Lost 5 men through enemy
artillery fire- 1 dead- 4 wounded-Very Cold- No sleep for
men who had to stay on alert- rain-Cold*

*10 Nov. 1944 :In the same positions-Spent day blasting into
the structures with C-2 charges-Secured the 1ˢᵗ or ground
floor of the fort- Sealed off the stairs and ran the enemy out.-
received some enemy artillery fire- No new developments-
Cold-rainy.*

*11 Nov. 1944 : Spent morning in the same positions,
blowing more of the initial fortress then organized for an
attack on the west concrete Barracks Bldg. Went out on a
frontal attack , but had to change tactics & hit it from the
roof. Took Lt. Ross and a few men , including four
engineers with C-2 , on the roof. Got into a heavy*

firefight with the enemy, but managed to drop the charges which were effective. After the situation "cooled off", Lt. Ross & I went back on top with 10 gals. of gas & two more sacks of C-2, poured gas into ventilating shaft, and then dropped in the W.P. grenades. Got burned. The iten. was o.k. and we blew in the front with the two charges- We took this position, then moved on to the 4-100mm gun positions, blew some more, then contacted 2nd Bn elements who were on the other side. They had captured all the men that we ran out of the fort. The fort was entirely ours then- We moved down into the town of Basse- Ham for the night. Cold Rainy-Lost 2 more men (wounded

12 Nov. 1944 : *Spent day in position in town, resting up after 72 hours of no sleep. Moved out just before dark to positions on edge of town to outpost the town. Have what is left of the 2nd Plat. with us to help us do the job. Each squad set up in a bldg. Cold –Cloudy*

13 Nov. 1944 :*In the same position with the same mission. Put in recommendations for awards for Burch, Weingartner, Shoate, Radokovic . Bridge finally got in & vehicles are beginning to move over, 10th Armored is to come over tonight. Got some mail in today-First since moving into assembly area -No new developments-Cold-rainy-*

14 Nov. 1944:*In the same position with the same mission. Got orders to be prepared to move out this aft. Went back to Fort with Col. + Cpt. Blake to give story to correspondents & got some pictures made- Co moved out to positions in woods N. of _____Went into Rgt. Reserve- A very Cold & wet night spent on ground-No new developments-*

1944, Fort Koenigsmacker West Barracks

Chapter Eighteen

The Rest of the Story, Day 1

2014, Fort Koenigsmacker Entry Gate

Butch's brevity in the diary left a lot of questions. This is the rest of the story . On the night of November 7-8, 1944 ,infantry and bridge building equipment was quietly moved up into the Cattenom forest.

Day 1: 9 Nov. ,1944 The Moselle was swollen seven times its normal width, which was a mixed blessing because the rafts floated over the extensive enemy laid minefields. The Germans were also lulled into thinking no one would be foolish enough to try a crossing under those flood conditions. Shortly after midnight on November 9th, in a cold , drizzling rain the G.I.'s picked up their boats in the village of Husange and carried their boats fifteen hundred yards through muddy, swampy fields and launched their boats. Men sunk up to their knees in the boggy fields, walked into submerged irrigation ditches and tripped over barbed wire fences until they arrived at the roaring river already exhausted.

About 1 a.m., a nearby explosion shattered the night. Caught in an exposed position, they believed their days to be numbered. The blast turned out to be from an American grenade. A pin had worked loose and the grenade detonated while still attached to a GI's chest-not a pretty sight. [37] Once they got to waist deep water, they struggled into their assault boats . The night was black and a cold wind whipped across the water.

The first waves crossed without many problems, but landed 1,000 yards further downstream than planned because of the increasing river current. There was no previous artillery preparation so they could maintain the element of surprise.

---

[37] Winebrenner p11

Hobert Winebrenner describes his crossing: " Once out in the water , we spun in circles , around and around . Between the downpour and the darkness, it was difficult to discern why. Our vessel turned like a top as it rapidly swept downstream. I felt my way forward to discover that the guys on one side were paddling like crazy, while those on the other had hunkered down. Experienced seaman we were not."[38]

A positive result of the flooding was that German waterfront foxholes were flooded and empty. Landing without detection by any Germans, the first three waves secured a muddy beachhead, capturing many German outpost defenders at bayonet point. The Germans were completely surprised.

Company A formed on the railroad track. Company C formed and prepared for its assigned attack on Basse - Ham. Unfortunately, there was a mix-up when the third wave's turn to cross came. The engineers assigned to man the boats and assist them across thought their job was done and left the area, After an hour delay, the third figured they were getting no engineering help and manned their boats by themselves , crossed and organized with the first two waves. Companies A and B were ready to attack the fort at daybreak.

---

[38] Winebrenner p12

The fourth wave (with elements of 1st battalion 358th, and the 2nd Battalion 359th) waited for the engineers to notify them and getting no word sent scouts forward to see what the delay was in crossing. They found the remainder of the boats sitting empty on the shore. The fourth wave did not commence crossing until 0715. They were greeted by wide-awake Germans, who began to shell and machine gun the troops crossing the river. Dozens of American soldiers were killed on the river by the German artillery, but most of the boats lost were swept out of control downstream by the wild rampaging river.

In the 358th sector, eighty original assault boats dwindled to twenty. The surviving infantry after reaching shore advanced to the shelter of the nearby woods. Meanwhile, Companies A and B had moved out stealthily in column to the woods surrounding the fort and waited in skirmish line for the coordinated assault time which was 0715. " There is always such a feeling of loneliness in the infantry. There seem to be so few of you in one place. There is a strange, disquieting feeling of being alone – alone with enemy and with death."[39]

Engineering units were working like beavers to expand the bridgehead with a pontoon bridge to allow tanks and reinforcements to cross the Moselle. Courageously, and eventually under constant fire they meshed together a

_____

[39] McConahey p 94

pontoon bridge across the river. Trucks carrying
bridge equipment were blown to bits by German
artillery fire. Wounded were moved to the rear as the
bridge advanced.

At dawn, the roaring, swirling, foamy Moselle River
sided with the Germans . The bridge was ripped apart
and swept down river. The six infantry battalions
across the river were on their own. The engineers
immediately went to work to improvise a cable lifeline
that would tow across basic supplies. At daybreak,
Fort Koeningsmacker zeroed in on the bridgehead
with everything it had. Americans were hugging the
ground or their foxholes under the relentless German
bombardment. The bridgehead was on the brink of
failure unless Fort Koeningsmacker could be
silenced.[40]

Butch's Company A of the 358th regiment was given
the responsibility to take the fort directly. Company B
was to flank the right side and Company C was to
attack the village of Basse-Ham on the left or
northwest side of the fort's base. Company C
commenced their attack in the night and cleared the
village of resistance by daylight with the exception of a
few snipers who were eventually eliminated. There
was no response from the fort so apparently there had
been no communication about the attack on Basse –
Ham.

---

[40] Note : Some accounts state that the four guns at Fort
Koenigsmacker were not operational and that the shelling came from
positions behind the fort guided by artillery observers in the fort.

2014, Fort Koenigsmacker , one of four Gun Turrets

Companies A and B commenced their assault with two platoons side by side. They charged over barbed wire and advanced up a gradual incline that got steeper and steeper. They arrived at the obstacle of a barbed wire filled moat. A path was snipped through the wire and the company crawled through the moat with artillery fire slamming all around them. Company A heard small arms fire from the right side so they knew Company B was close to the German trenches on that side. The Germans in the trenches in front of Company A appeared unaware that Company A was just down the slope from them.

Butch, leader of the first platoon led a few picked scouts up the slope toward the main observation post on the crest. Shells were still falling all around them as they advanced ducking into every available shell-hole for shelter on the way. Without a scratch, they reached the crest and dropped into the German trench. The Germans figured that it would be nuts for anyone to be out in that shell fire so they had posted only a few men in the trench system while the rest hunkered down underground safe from the artillery fire.

At approximately 0900, German mortars and artillery were raining fire on the fort and on the village of Bass -Ham down below. The American troops in the town took shelter in the building basements.

The job of reducing the main fort would fall on Company A and Company B ,who were being bloodied by the enemy mortar and artillery fire falling on the fort. Observers from the armored observation post were directing the mortar fire. It needed to be eliminated before an attack could advance. This part of the attack was led by Lt. Neil and Lt. Patrick from Company A and Lt. Martin with the attached engineers.

Lt. Harris Neil, Co. A , 358th Inf. : " When my platoon reached the parapet, we surprised a group of five or six Jerries. One jumped for a machine gun and the sergeant killed him- fortunately. The others ran off down a trench and started throwing hand grenades. So for a little while we had quite a hand grenade battle, mostly with us throwing their grenades back at them.

Up to that time we had lost no men, but with daylight they opened up on us with machine guns from the other side of the Fort and with artillery and mortars. Those guns were zeroed in on the trenches and it was not so good, and we began to have casualties. Anyway, we were on top of the Fort. Sort of a queer position. You scratch your head and say, Now what the hell do I do next? Our job was to get the Jerries underground and keep them there. We wanted to get them underground while we stayed on top and then to blast them out of one part of the Fort to another. We aimed to drive them from this side to the other and then out, and that's what we did." With the growing morning light, the rounded steel top of the armored observation turret came into view forty yards away. A bazooka was used on it a couple of times. They hoped the German observer had ducked. Lt. Neil signaled for the rest of the Company A platoons to rush the slope while Pfc. Edward Singer of Philadelphia dropped a smoke grenade into the turret slits. Lt. William Kilpatrick, Paris, Texas , 3rd platoon and Lt. William Silberberg, Westbury, Long Island, 2nd platoon led their platoons through the smoke screen right into Germans moving to drive the Americans off the fort. The Americans littered the area with dead Germans as they occupied the trenches and nearest concrete shelters. Lt. Neil's platoon joined with them and by 1000 the Americans controlled the top of Fort Koeningsmacker.

At this time, the Germans directed mortar fire on the American held positions. Heavy casualties were suffered by the platoons. Private Carl Weingartner, North Wales, Penn, medic for Company A used up his supplies patching up the wounded. The Americans drove off three counterattacks during the rainy afternoon and a fourth was stopped by American artillery. American casualties were piling up and the men sweated out Day one praying for a break. Butch's platoon discovered a ramp that was not on his maps. It led to a doorway in a massive concrete wall in which four gun slits were cut. The ramp went down about 30 feet and was about 20 feet wide. They hoped to gain entry to the interior of the Fort. Butch did not know if the gun slits were manned, but decided to take a chance. He slid down and slung three satchels of explosive into the doorway and blew it off near a door hinge. When the door blew off,it revealed a second inner three-inch thick steel door six feet in and two feet to the right. Luckily, the Germans were using this area behind the first door as a storeroom and had piled supplies up so much they could not use the gun slits. The platoon slid down the ramp and entered the passageway. Every time the Americans tried to get into the passageway, the Germans fired a burp gun from under the door. Then Butch sneaked in and stuffed explosive satchels under the door. He commented " That explosion was tremendous. It not only blew out the door and wrecked everything inside, but smoke and dust puffed out through ventilators and doors all over the place." They then got into the passageway and got to the stairs and dumped more explosives, knocking out the stairs " I figured we had driven them out of this section of the fort".

The western portion of the fort was worked on with explosives for the remainder of the day. By the end of the day, the Americans had systematically knocked out the observation port here and the sally and shelter points. Company A had overrun about 1/3 of the fort. The Germans withdrew into inner areas of the fort and called for mortar fire on the attackers. The Americans were forced back to the original positions in the trenches and sustained 40 casualties on day one. Company B had been stuck on the south portion of the fort It was ordered to move from its present position during the night and to join Company A where the greatest progress was being made. The weather continued to be cold and rainy and they spent the night on top of the fort under fire until dawn. They had used up all of their high explosives and wanted more of this brand new stuff called " composition C2".

Planning for the action had relied on the transport of supplies across a floating bridge to be built across the river. The river had a normal width of 300-350 feet. By noon, it had grown to a width of 2,400 feet. Engineers started their bridge construction in knee-deep water that grew to waist deep. The current caused bridging operations to completely cease. The flooding river cut off all reinforcements and supplies. At the end of the day, seven towns and villages had been cleared and the bridgehead was six miles wide by two miles deep in some places.

The village of Basse -Ham had fallen to Co. C.
Companies A & B had reached the fort and were
learning how to blow the Germans from their positions.
The heavy American casualties were being treated in
the aid station that had crossed and set up in Basse
Ham. Six battalions of infantry were across the river
attacking armored and fortified positions with hand
carried weapons. The river continued to rise. As night
came, the Americans had meager supplies of
ammunition, medical supplies and rations. Wounded
needed to be evacuated. Emergency resupply was
necessary and it began that night. All available
personnel were utilized in an effort led by
Lt.Sheridan,Lt. Martin, and Lt. Autrey. They loaded
boats and rowed them across all night. Critical
supplies were thus replenished to the battalion
through this persistent effort. Many boats overturned
so the wounded were deemed safer where they were.
A bridge was critically needed.

The enemy reaction to the attack by the 90th was slow
in regards to reinforcements because they were taken
by surprise and because the attack fortunately hit a
seam between the 19th and the 416th VG Divisions
causing command confusion in German HQ . The
decision to supply German reinforcement of the area
was delayed.

Chapter Nineteen

The Rest of the Story, Day 2

Day 2: 10 November,1944. By the next morning ,
Company B moved around and took over the left half
of the former position Company A held on Day 1.
Germans had come back into the town cutting off a
platoon of Company C in the southwest end of Basse-
Ham during the night. The Germans occupied houses
southwest of a stream that ran through Basse- Ham. Lt.
Charles Watson, an observer for Canon Company
climbed a church steeple just above the German
positions. He directed fire that took out the Germans at
risk of being hit by his own directed fire. His action
and the accurate artillery fire relieved the trapped
platoon.

At the Fort, more explosives were needed, but there
was still no bridge. Heroically, five piper cub scout
planes heavily loaded down flew through the storm
and heavy anti-aircraft fire to drop fresh satchel
charges to the Americans on top of the fort.

Back at Fort Koenigsmacker, Companies A and B resumed action. Butch's Company A consolidated and took the right half of what had been their zone the day before. They knocked out all of the armored fort top observation posts in their area with "C2" and blasted their way into two inner tunnels that provided some shelter. The Germans slowly withdrew back into the fort. Resistance was harsh and persistent. The Germans continued to rain mortar fire on the attackers and casualties continued to mount. A and B Companies had worked their way to a central position on the fort's top near where they thought the enemy guns were emplaced. They were on the edge of the concrete west barracks.

2014, Fort Koenigsmacker, Vent

Lt. Neil was hugging the grass on top of the fort when he wondered what would happen if they got gasoline down one of the ventilator shafts in the underground bunker. He and Lt. Ross, while ducking enemy machine gun fire crawled on their bellies to the ventilator shaft and pulled it off. Lt. Neil poured 10 gallons of gas down it. Lt. Ross tossed white phosphorous grenades into the shaft. There was the sound of an explosion and screams from within the bunker. A body was seen blown out an open ventilator shaft. Suddenly, fire blackened screaming Germans were fleeing the barracks from side doors . Lt. Neil ran past them to another ventilator and dropped an explosive inside. Flames exploded and spurted from more vents and gun turrets. Immediately, this deadly technique was adopted on the rest of the fort.   They ran out of explosives again by the end of the day. The enemy had retreated deeper into the fort as they were driven back. As the pressure from the Americans ebbed from lack of explosives, the determined defenders crept back into the abandoned positions. Five planes again provided new explosives dropped directly into battalion positions. The Company continued its destruction of the German positions. Company A got into the interior of some of the bunkers and tunnels , but was blocked by rubble from their destruction. They opted to continue the operation from above although the captured area did provide some shelter.

In the 359th zone, they were east of Malling by daybreak and had cut the highway from Thionville to Metz. The town of Malling was seized from the sleeping Germans in a matter of minutes. The 2nd Battalion was on the southeast side of the fort pinned down. The 3rd Battalion had slipped past the fort onto the Elzange Ridge overlooking the fort. They surprised 150 Germans moving up to reinforce the fort and took them prisoner.

Back at the fort, on the evening of Day 2, a 50 man German counterattack launched from the northeast corner of the fort. The 1st Battalion yielded no ground in the repulse of the attack. Twenty-eight Germans lay dead as the remainder limped back to cover.

The Moselle River continued to rise until it was 1 ½ miles wide. No bridge could be built yet and supplies had to be shuttled. Evacuation of the most critically wounded was finally accomplished with great difficulty by boat.

Chapter Twenty

Day 3, "This Fort is Ours"

Day 3: 11 November. Day three dawns with Fort Koeningsmacker still not conquered. The river was still rising steadily from the rain and no bridge was in place. German reinforcements thought to be nearby were bound to move in soon. Everyone in the 90th now knew the situation was grave for the eight battalions across the river unsupported by armor. The only support available was from artillery working from the opposite bank and firing around the clock. Casualties were mounting from enemy fire and from fighting for two days and nights in rain and mud without blankets and on reduced cold rations. The planes had delivered new satchel charges to the men on top of the fort.

" How those soldiers ever lasted out I'll never know, isolated as they were. They had no overcoats, raincoats or blankets to protect from the cold and the driving rain; they had no overshoes to keep their feet dry in the deep mud; very little food or ammunition. Yet those boys stood fast against the fury of desperate counterattacks, threw back the enemy and advanced across heavily mined fields in the face of fanatical resistance." [41]

---

[41] McConahey p 95

Around noon, Lt. Neil and Lt. Ross were preparing their men for an attack against a door of the fort when a muddy messenger from Divisional Headquarters delivered the order to pull back to a bearded and red-eyed Lt. Neil. Butch showed the order to Lt. Ross. They understood that the order was justified as Company A at that moment could claim only about sixty fighters out of the original 186 and that was if you counted the lightly wounded. Lt. Neil immediately made a decision with the concurrence of Lt. Ross. Butch scribbled a message to headquarters:

"This Fort is ours – until my platoon is down to two men. Then and only then will we retire. I could not ask my men to leave here now. They are more determined than I to finish the job."[42] [43]

The assault was resumed with vigor and the Germans were squeezed and blown into an even smaller area of the fort through the use of gasoline, grenades, and "C2". The German garrison had been pushed back into the eastern barracks another concrete stronghold like the west barracks, but without ventilators. This position was under the big guns. On the face of the east barracks was a garage .Lt. Rex Ross, St. Joseph, Missouri blew a door half off of it's hinges and was met with machine gun fire from inside the turret. Lt. Neil sneaked up to the door and set off another blast that blew in the door. Eight Germans lay dead in the tunnel behind the door.

---

[42] Barnes p 6 of The Assault chapter
[43] Huss, Cosmopolitan p 28

"You never saw such an explosion, " Lt. Neil said. "There was a Jerry over there- in the door opening into the trench and that explosion blew him out the door as though he had been shot out of a popgun. We got them out of the east barracks and out of the fort and they came out and surrendered to the other company which arrived in back of the fort that morning."

The Americans invaded the tunnel and heard the sound of retreating Germans . Company C had filtered into the fort from Basse -Ham during the night, after repulsing a counterattack there, so that all that was left of the First Battalion was at the fort.

The Americans were moving in to finish the Germans.

Company C, captured a pillbox which turned out to be a link into a main passageway underneath the fort. They pushed into it and proceeded to attack the Germans within. At 1600, dozens of Germans fled to the rear of the fort via a tunnel that ran 400 yards on the northeast corner of the fort and down the slope where Company G, 2nd Battalion was waiting for them. Germans were rapidly gunned down. Suddenly white flags were waved from various points of the fort. Three hundred and seventy-two wide-eyed Germans stumbled out with their hands held high. It is estimated that 128 Germans were killed at Koenigsmacker. 1st Battalion lost 21 killed, 85 wounded and five missing. Fort Koenigsmacker , conquered by the 90th Division was the only one of the Metz type fortifications to be successfully taken by storm.

Chapter Twenty-one

As the Smoke Cleared

The capture of Fort Koenigsmacker lifted the morale of the 90th and they pushed into the enemy with new energy. The Germans launched a series of counterattacks for the rest of the third and then the fourth day. They were repelled by American artillery and rifle fire and hundreds more German prisoners were taken. On the fifth day, the Moselle River , finally siding with the Americans dropped an inch an hour and the engineers completed a bridge by midnight at Malling. Tanks and trucks rolled over the river. The Germans were pushed back to the east and all connections to Metz were severed. The trap was complete.

12 November saw Butch's 1st Battalion moved to regimental reserve covering the right flank of the division and resting up after Ft. Koenigsmacker. Company C secured the fort. Company B occupied the area between Basse -Ham and the fort and Company A held Basse- Ham covering the flank of the regiment.

At a severely high cost, the Tough 'Ombres of the First
Battalion had overcome one of the strongest positions ever
designed by German engineering and defeated Nazi troops
under orders to hold their post at all costs. Lt. Harris Neil was
awarded the Distinguished Service Cross by command of Lt.
General George Patton for "extraordinary heroism " in
connection with this operation. He also received a Purple
Heart for severe burns , the French Croix de Guerre , Etoile
d'Argent (silver star for heroism) .Patton called a press
conference after the event to talk about the capture of
Koenigsmacker. He characterized it as one of the greatest
events in the war.

On the 12 November, the 90th Division commander, General
Van Fleet was promoted to Major General. [44]

A letter of commendation from Lt. General G.S. Patton Jr. to
the commanding general, 90th infantry division contained the
following remark: " The capture and development of your
bridgehead over the Moselle River in the vicinity of
Koenigsmacker will ever rank as one of the epic river
crossings of history."

In 2013, Fort Koeningsmacker was recognized for its historic
importance and the site was partially cleaned up and made
available to the public.

---

[44] Cole p.416

A critique of the Koenigsmacker operation by Captain Henry Barnes in training course materials used at Fort Benning, Georgia is summarized as follows:

This operation was well planned and commanders had time to make a thorough reconnaissance. Troops were properly oriented and briefed. The wild card that almost spelled disaster was the unanticipated rise of the Moselle River. Perhaps more information could have been gathered beforehand from locals, but this might have tipped off the Germans. One setback was the lack of coordination of the 179th Engineer Battalion when the assault boats were left unmanned by the engineers at the river for the fourth wave. Fortunately, the fourth wave took the initiative to cross without benefit of engineers. The entire credit for the success of the assault on Fort Koenigsmacker goes to the skill, guts and daring of each individual "dogface".

Chapter Twenty-two

Advance

On November 12, 1944, bridging at Cattenom and Malling was progressing. The Moselle River was ebbing and support armor was being ferried across. Each company was in need of replacements to make up for losses and there were still no dry clothes or blankets for coping with the frigid nights. The bridge at Cattenom was completed on the morning of November 13, but the ebbing Moselle revealed a large German minefield that took five hours to clear. Finally by dawn of November 14 , the 90th Division had crossed all support units across the river and for the first time in six days and nights, the troops in the bridgehead had overcoats, blankets and dry socks.[45]

Butch's First Battalion of the 358th Infantry was placed in reserve covering the right flank of the division and resting after Ft. Koenigsmacker. The 2nd and 3rd battalions commenced an attack against Valmestroff and Elzange. These villages were stiffly defended by the Germans, but fell to the Americans. The Germans introduced a new deadly plastic and wood boxed mine to the 90th here. Engineers could not detect them with their mine detectors.

---

[45] Cole p 400

On November 13, mines slowed the 358th Infantry down as it advanced along the ridge chain.

November, 15 revealed that the 90th Division bridgehead had attained a width of eleven miles and a depth of seven miles. [46] At daybreak on November 15, three battalions of German infantry, field artillery , tanks, and assault guns, were sent around the open right flank of the 358th Infantry to an assembly area in the Bois de Stuckange. They struck east at Distroff with a vicious counterattack that hit the 2nd battalion, 358th infantry breaching its outpost line and moving into the streets of Distroff. The Americans were pushed back into the buildings by swarms of German infantry and armor. They clung to the village even calling for artillery fire on the streets of the town around them. A platoon of tanks was sent for reinforcement and reached the north edge of the town. Colonel Clarke , the regimental commander ordered his only infantry reserve the 1st Battalion to move up from Fort Koenigsmacker to the Inglange-Distroff road, so that it could move to the aid of the 2nd or the 3rd Battalion that was under heavy German artillery fire. However, the Germans had been broken after a four-hour fight and retreated along the road to Metzervisse. The Distroff counterattack was the last to strike the 90th Division during the envelopment of Metz.

[46] Cole p. 410

15 Nov. 1944 *:Moved out at dawn. Cross open terrain into another series of woods – cleaned them out. Slept out in the ditch- Very heavy sleet and ice- Cold & Sleet-*

16 Nov. 1944 *: Moved out at 0700 to woods near_____ where we cleaned them of Germans. & received very heavy enemy artillery fire. Five lost Manns, Simpson + Gorman & Anderson (dead) and had Harjo, Dunnyn, Reelich, Gilliard, Obeesick wounded- pulled out after dark and out posted road near* **Distroff.** *It was very cold & we had sleet during night-*

On 17 November, the 358th was moved forward to the right of the 357th while the 359th went into reserve. The 2nd Battalion with tanks out in front and in an attack coordinated with the 1st Battalion took Metzervisse after the village received heavy shelling and a flanking attack had turned the German position along the railroad embankment to the north. Metzervisse was quickly overrun and the 1st Battalion moved forward to a position on the Dalstein – Metz road. [47]. The Germans were pulling back to close a hole that was developing in the German front.

---

[47] Cole p 414

17 Nov. 1944 :Jumped off at dawn following C & B Co through woods- received heavy shell fire- Lost Manns & Burch . then made an assault across open field under very heavy (fire) to woods near _____ when we arrived there our own artillery came in and killed Klein & wounded Noto, Ferris, Radokovic also Capt. Blake- Spent night in these woods- Cold & Clear

On the 18 and 19th of November, the Americans were pursuing the retreating German columns. The 359th Infantry regiment was ordered by General Van Fleet to continue the pursuit thus relieving the tired 358th regiment. They were ordered to rest at Luttange. The rest of the Division carried out the general mission closing the gap east of Metz. The 359th now held Conde-Northen, twelve miles east of Metz and the 90th Reconnaissance Troop held Avancy, blocking one of the main escape routes from Metz. The Americans fired on any escaping Germans with all they had. On 19 November, the 359th cut off another Metz exit road at Les Etangs. Planes working with the infantry attacked the fleeing Germans. Germans were surrendering in droves. At 1030 the 90th Reconnaissance linked up with the 735th Tank Battalion supporting the 5th Division and the envelopment of Metz was complete.

Known losses during this operation were 2,100 German prisoners, 40 destroyed German tanks and assault guns, 75 destroyed German artillery pieces , 200 destroyed German vehicles and an unknown number of dead and wounded. The 90th Division had 2,300 casualties in the first seven days of the fighting. [48]

The battle for Metz tactically consisted of four parts, a preliminary demonstration by the 95th division, the wide envelopment north of Metz by the 90th Division and 10th Armored Division, a close proximity envelopment south of Metz by the 5th Division and a containing action west of the Moselle by the 95th Division culminating in a final assault on both sides of the Moselle river. [49] The Germans in Metz for all practical purposes capitulated on November 20, 1944 and resistance officially ended at 1435 on November 22. [50] A few outlying forts held on until 8 December. The credit for the success of the operation goes entirely to the ground forces as the air attacks were ineffective. The Germans carried out Hitler's orders and held on to delay the Americans. Strong positions, bad weather, floods, and their determined resistance aided them.

Now, that Metz had fallen, the mission of the 90th and the rest of XX Corps was to advance on the Saar River and onto German soil populated by defenders with the added motivation of defending their homeland.

---

[48] Cole p 416
[49] Cole p 421
[50] Cole p 447

Chapter Twenty-three

Paris

*18 Nov. 1944 : Moved through woods- met no enemy- moved into town of **Luttange** for the night-Spent night in barn- Cold & Clear.*

The days of November 19-20 were spent resting while they received replacements for their numerous casualties. They were trucked to the town of Malderm shortly after breakfast following the 10th Armored. The next day Butch received new orders. He was placed in charge of 38 enlisted men and 3 officers from the 358th. Their target this time was Paris for a needed leave. They assembled in two trucks and drove to a rear rest area for the night. At 0735 on November 23, they left the rest area and drove to Paris arriving at 1445 . They hit the town that night.

On the 23 November, while Butch was in Paris ,the 358th Regiment of the 90th Division (depleted to 63% of normal strength) was ordered to advance with the mission of capturing the villages of Sinz and Munzingen. They did so with artillery support through terrain covered by pillboxes and scarred by deep anti-tank ditches, which were crossed with ladders. 2nd battalion fell victim to short falling friendly tank fire and later was raked by machine gun fire coming from a bunker at the village of Oberleuken. 1st battalion was sent into Oberleuken where the fight went on into the night. 3rd battalion had become disorganized by a flamethrower armed German counterattack. They moved on to take the villages of Tettingen and Butzdorf pillbox by pillbox. Tettingen was the scene of a tank led counterattack against K Company of the 358th who clung to their toehold in the village as the German tank and bazooka fire blew away the houses they were occupying. American tanks finally relieved them. There was a house-to-house battle for Oberlaeuken by the 1st Battalion. 2nd battalion advanced to the top of a hill five hundred yards northwest of Oberleuken. Because of heavy casualties, 2nd Battalion now consisted of less than 100 men.

This entire three-day battle to penetrate what was called the Orscholz line reduced the combat strength of the 358th infantry to 40%. [51] The exhausted 358th infantry was in no shape to continue moving forward and was relieved by the 10th Armored Division .The 358th had made the deepest penetration of the Orscholz line that would be made in 1944. The depleted regiment now went into 90th Division reserve at Veckring Barracks north of Dalstein. Colonel Clarke had to be hospitalized with pneumonia and many new replacements needed further training.

---

[51] Cole p497

On the morning of November 24, Butch slept until 0900 when he arose for breakfast. He then spent the day Christmas shopping , site seeing and photographing the city. That night, he and some of the guys took in a stage show at the Olympia. His men back in battle were on his mind because he tracked their progress towards the Sarre River during his time in Paris.

At 1030 on November 25, the guys left Paris and drove to a rest area near Thionville where they spent the night . The next day he joined his company near Oberperl. He sent out a squad with the engineers and they blew up a German pillbox while being shelled by the enemy. The next day, November 27, saw Butch in position at some barracks at Wehingen where they set up camp. A couple of days later, he went with a group to Metz to attend a ceremony. He was experiencing stomach ailments at this time. December 1, saw the 358th still resting at Wehingen. They got paid on December 1 for their work in November. It was not nearly enough compensation for what they had endured.

1944, German Pillbox after attack by Butch's platoon

Chapter Twenty- Four

Another River

On December 3rd, the officers were briefed about another possible river crossing. They stayed in this location until December 4th when they motored to the town of St. Barbara inside Germany. At 1400, they pulled out and took up an outpost position on a hill overlooking the Saar River near Wallerfangen. It was raining and sleeting most of day and clear and cold during the night. On December 5th, as the cold rain continued, they prepared for a river crossing scheduled for the next day. At 0330, they jumped off and crossed over at 0430. Butch's diary says that they took their objective on the outer edge of Dillingen. They out posted next to a railroad and he noted that there were two casualties with 1 man killed (Miller) 1 wounded (Butzmann).

December had arrived with even more cold and wet weather and the occasional snow flurry. On Dec. 2, the 358th Infantry, now under command of Lt. Col. F.H. Loomis was ordered to be ready to move from the Veckring training ground, where it was rehabbing and taking on replacements, to a forward position on the right wing of the Division in the vicinity of the German towns of Dillingen and Pachten on the Sarre River's east side and near St. Barbara on the west side . They were ordered by General Walker to cross the Saar River as early as possible and to take Dillingen in one of the strongest and widest parts of the Siegfried line where it came down to the edge of the river. The attack was set for the early morning of Dec. 6. The terrain in the area is hilly with scattered forests. As one approaches the Saar River, you head down into a river valley. The Dillingen area was part of the German West Wall, the last barrier of defense for Nazi Germany. Dillingen itself was fortress studded with many camouflaged pillboxes. Your local jewelry store would turn out to be a steel and concrete pillbox.[52] The job for the G.I.'s was to clear a path through the defenses for the tanks. For 16 days and nights, the Americans hit over and over again at the enemy's fortifications. Supplies and rations were ferried across the river on every boat available. The enemy was driven out of pillbox after pillbox.

The Saar River normally about 200 feet wide was flooded. Across the river, the West Wall defenses began at the bank and continued eastward. There were pillboxes and trenches laid throughout the area to an unknown depth. The mission of the 358th was to capture Pachten and Dillingen, one of the most fortified areas of the West Wall , then block any enemy approach along the valley of the Prims. [53]Little was known about German strength. Butch's 1st Battalion, 358th (Maj. A.L. Nichols) gathered at the river north of Wallerfangen and crossed the river silently in assault boats at 0430 in pre-dawn darkness along with other regiments. Artillery from the 359th opened up way to the left to draw German attention away from the vulnerable assault boats.

---

[52] McConahey p 99
[53] Cole p 560

Surprise was complete except in the area of the 357th infantry near Rehlingen. Enemy guns and mortars and machine gun fire met the advancing troops. American artillery opened fire pounding the German battery positions . The Americans advanced across the flats east of the river pillbox by pillbox. The 357th regiment to the left was able to advance about 1 ½ miles. Most of the infantry on the right were pinned down.

Butch's 358th Regiment, 1st Battalion successfully moved toward Pachten, a suburb of Dillingen along a road north of the Prims River. They encountered little opposition until they reached the railroad tracks at the east edge of Dillingen. [54] Hitler ordered the 719th Division, with ten tanks and some tank destroyers from the 11th Panzer Division, to destroy the 90th Division bridgehead in the Dillingen-Pachten area. They arrived and went into action on 7th December. [55] They first attacked positions held by the 358th, 3rd Battalion at the edge of Pachten. The Americans broke up the attack and the 3rd Battalion organized a firm defensive line west of the railroad tracks. 2nd Battalion cleared pillboxes in the center while 1st Battalion held the right. At the close of 7 December, there was no vehicular bridge across the Saar because of German artillery and the flooding river. The Americans would take pillboxes and then lose them back to the Germans and then the Americans would retake them.

---

[54] Cole p 563
[55] Cole p566

The initiative had slipped to the Germans by 8 December and they counter-attacked harassing the 2nd and 3rd battalions of the 358th infantry continuously. Substantial losses were inflicted on the Germans. 1st battalion continued their eastward attack across the railroad tracks where they were hit by fire from warehouses along the track and driven back. The railroad station across the track was later taken by C Company. Further south, Butch and his fellow 1st battalion troops fought into the municipal slaughterhouse, west of the railroad. Its position was considered tactically important because of its position on the right flank of the 358th.

The 357th regiment on the left was counter-attacked hard. The enemy was repulsed with heavy losses to both sides during hand-to-hand fighting. The situation was deemed critical due to the weakened battalions and the lines were ordered to be shortened.

Company A soon found itself in a "prime " location.

8 Dec. 1944 :Moved out at 0900 & attacked the slaughter house area- knocked out two pill boxes- captured 6 men- One of our men wounded (Strong) Set up positions in slaughter factory- White & Cpt. Baid left to go back to states for 3 months- I took over command of A Co. Received some enemy Artillery fire -Cold + Rainy.

"We caught wind that there was an enormous slaughterhouse open for business in our sector of the city. Dressed pork halves and huge quarters of beef packed the cooling room. …we helped ourselves to all we could carry."[56]

On 9 December, General Van Fleet committed his reserves, the 359th Infantry to the Dillingen bridgehead fight with hopes of breaking the stalemate. They were to move between the 358th and 357th to eliminate the enemy salient separating the 357th an 358th. This salient was a line of fortified positions that projected perpendicular to the river. They advanced with new energy, but while they took pressure off the 357th and took some pillboxes , they did not succeed in destroying the heavily fortified German salient between the regiments.

The 357th regiment's position was becoming more critical by the hour. The 358th regiment continued its fight along the railroad tracks in Dillingen. 3rd battalion, 358th blasted enemy houses with a captured gun, the 90th's only artillery piece east of the river. 2nd Battalion, 358th, failed in an assault across the tracks. One company (F) got across when they discovered a tunnel, but they were cut off or captured on the other side. 1st battalion, 358th received heavy counter-attacks by forces that outnumbered them. The battle raged back and forth in the slaughterhouse area buildings resulting in a stalemate.

---

[56] Winebrenner p 12

Late afternoon 9 December, the first light anti-tank guns and the first tank crossed the river by ferry, but they could not help the 357th on the left because of the remaining German salient that separated the 358th from the 357th. Supplies were dropped to the 357th by air and two hundred replacements arrived.

9 Dec. 1944: *Same positions with mission of holding- Rainy- During day   the Artillery & Cannon Co. worked on pillboxes + factory area in order to soften it up for the Inf. No new developments except quite a good deal of M.G. fire from River on our positions in the large Pill box-Cold & rainy*

10 Dec. 1944 : *Same positions with same mission. Got a counter- attack at 1745 this afternoon- Lost all contact with 2 & 3 platoons for entire night- One man wounded seriously (Shoate) another slightly hit. - Rainy- Cold + very critical situation.*

On 10 December, the Germans counter-attacked with the largest attack to date all along the line. The 358th's 1st Battalion , Company A, (Lt. Neil) was hit and surrounded by a very strong enemy force that intended to retake the slaughterhouse area. Butch's company was reported lost when telephone communications were severed. However, this was not true because the position was in American hands at the end of the day. Late in the day, the Germans formed east of the tracks for an assault. A and B companies dashed across the tracks counter-attacking the Germans by wheeling left through a cemetery and into a fortified church on the enemy flank. The Germans were surprised and the planned attack was broken up. At dark, the Americans withdrew from their position. [57]

The 357th repelled assault after assault against it. The 359th fought a seesaw battle in the pillboxes. 3rd Battalion fought it's way into the German fortified salient trying to link up with the 1st battalion 358th, but by night had lost all organization and was isolated by squads and platoons. Supplies were brought over by assault boat because the Germans destroyed the ferry.

11 Dec. 1944 : *Same positions with same mission. Regained contact with all platoons & found that we still had control of entire slaughter house- We left Pillbox, but again got control of it. Situation is same as first day here- The company had a total of 3 casualties during the attack. None were too serious- Got in two new officers during night Lt. Gormley for (2nd platoon) & Lt. Anderson to (3rd) platoon. Cold & Rainy*

---

[57] Cole p583

On 11 December, the 357th withdrew it's lines in the north and northeast. The 358th and 359th probed for a corridor through the pesky German salient and linked up at 1530 via a lateral corridor obtained by accurate artillery fire, infantry assaults and psychological warfare. A Luxembourger succeeded in convincing five pillboxes to surrender. The ferry was repaired and tanks began crossing the river. The 358th turned towards Dillingen and artillery opened up on it. General Van Fleet wanted the town for cover from the winter cold and rain. [58]

12 Dec. 1944 *:Same positions with same mission. No new developments. Spent time firing on enemy positions with Artillery. Received some enemy Artillery (slight) & some M.G. Fire- Cold + Rain.*

13 Dec. 1944 *:Same positions with same missions. More firing on enemy with Artillery. Received more M.G. Fire- from Pillboxes etc.- No new developments during the night. Cold + Cloudy*

14 Dec. 1944 *:Same positions with same mission.. Spent day firing on enemy spots with Artillery. Got attack order for 15 Dec- No new developments -Cold + Cloudy*

By 15 December, the Germans had withdrawn all but rearguard elements from the Saarlautern-Dillingen area because the offensive by the American 7th army along the west bank of the Rhine had gained momentum and

---

[58] Cole p 586

threatened to break through the West wall in the weak Wissembourg sector. [59]

15 Dec. 1944 : The Bn. Jumped off on the attack at 0730 this morning. We started out on our phase of the attack at 1545- Crossed tracks, went through cemetery- cleared factory bldgs. & blew pill boxes- Set up defensive positions here for the night- No casualties during the operation-No new developments -Cold + Cloudy

This attack moved under a smoke screen and the 358th fought their way under heavy enemy fire into the streets and houses of Dillingen followed closely by tanks and tank destroyers. The Germans broke after a few hours. By night, the 358th had cleared the buildings for a distance of three hundred yards east of the railroad tracks. The 359th gained 500 yards encountering moderate resistance. There was no counter-attack from the weakened Germans.

16 Dec. 1944 : In the same positions with same mission.. Improved our positions – Searched out all areas & set up better defenses. No new developments - Cold + Cloudy

17 Dec. 1944: In the same position with same mission No new developments - Cold + Cloudy

On 18 December, 3rd Battalion, 359th Infantry and 2nd Battalion, 358th Infantry made a cautious coordinated drive into Dillingen. Within 3 hours, Dillingen was primarily in American possession.

---

[59] Cole p 587

The capture of Dillingen, a bloody urban brawl had put a large hole in the mighty German West Wall (Siegfried Line) and everyone thought the allies were about to punch through Germany and end the war.

Chapter Twenty- Five

Withdrawal

On 19 Dec., Patton ordered the evacuation of the hard won territory around Dillingen. The 90th Division bridgehead was to be evacuated. Third Army needed to shift its divisions toward the Ardennes. The Battle of the Bulge was taking center stage. In October, General Bradley's American First Army had captured its first German city, Aachen, Germany. They advanced into the snow-covered Hurtgen Forest sustaining heavy casualties.

Hitler unleashed a bold attack named "Watch on the Rhine". It was an "all in " commitment of 24 of his best Divisions and masses of armor. The goal was to pierce the Allied lines in the Ardennes Forest and roll on to Antwerp, thus cutting American supply lines and hopefully demoralizing the Allies into a position from where they could negotiate a peace settlement. Then, the Germans could turn their attention back on the approaching Russians .

On 16 December, at 0500, eight Panzer Divisions, under cover of fog rolled out of the forest and broke through the Allied lines along a 70-mile front in Belgium and Luxembourg. The support of the 90th Division was urgently needed and they were ordered to shift towards Bastogne The battle would become known as the Battle of the Bulge because of the early forty-mile wide by sixty-mile deep bend in the Allied lines. The Germans rolled over the American lines until they met stubborn resistance from the American 101st Airborne Division at the crossroads town of Bastogne, Belgium. The Germans could not dislodge the 101st and squandered resources and time trying to take this position. The Americans held, and the fog lifted. Allied air power then had a field day with German tanks. Hitler's gamble had failed and the Germans retreated on foot as they were out of fuel.

December 20, 1944 saw Butch back in position at the slaughterhouse where he notes that they relieved "K" Company. The next afternoon, they took up positions along the railroad tracks to form a thin screening force for the withdrawal of the rest of the battalion, who were crossing the river at 0700. We all fully expected to mop up the remaining German resistance, then move out of Dillingen and onto the next adventure, but it never happened. A runner banged the door to announce , "We're backing out of Dillingen, tonight." Dillingen was ours and now, we were handing it back to the Germans ? What of the sacrifice ? Was it all in vain ? [60] This was the first time this battalion ever gave ground and even though it was a strategic retreat rather than tactical, it still hurt.

During the December battle on the Saar, the 90th had lost more than one third of its strength due to KIA, wounded, MIA and sick. [61] There was still no bridge over the Saar River for the nine infantry battalions and about 100 vehicles. It took three nights to move them across.

---

[60] Winebrenner p175
[61] Cole p 589

Hobert Winebrenner discussed the withdrawal across the Saar :

" A shadowy outline of men disappeared into the darkness. Single file, they sidled to the Saar. What the engineers labeled a footbridge, I called a living nightmare. A fiery descent straight to hell would be less intimidating. A tenuous mix of cork slabs and aluminum channel, it danced to many tunes. And in the darkness, you couldn't actually see it. Only the luminous tape led the way. Lets just say that the river wasn't the only thing getting my pants wet. "[62]

At 1040 on 22 December, Lt. Neil and the rear guard arrived on the west bank. American guns smashed Pachten and Dillingen with round after round. During December, the

---

[62] Winebrenner p 176

90th had captured 1,298 prisoners and killed scores. The 90th lost 239 killed, 924 wounded and approximately 440 missing. Over 1,000 troops were evacuated because of sickness. [63]

Numerous casualties came from trench foot,which got its name in WWI, and is caused by wet feet. The feet become numb from lack of circulation and begin to swell. There are blisters, sores, fungal infections and feet can be lost. Men that could not walk were often carried to forward positions. Butch like many suffered from trench foot. It was solved by having dry socks and the army starting pushing dry clothing and foot care to reduce the problem. Butch also suffered from frostbite from freezing temperatures because they were not issued proper winter gear for a long time due to logistics.

22 Dec. 1944: *Pulled out of screening positions & crossed river at 0400. Moved on foot to St.Barbara. then on to Wallertangen where we got trucks at 0900 & moved to town of Launstonf where we went into Regt. Reserve. Set up in the town. Cold & snow*

December 23- January brought no movement for the Battalion from the Wallertangen area other than scouting positions for delaying defensive purposes in case of German attack. Butch had his men dig in their positions on Christmas Eve where they hunkered down for a cold and clear night. They celebrated Christmas dinner the next day, finished prepping their defenses and took it easy most of the day. The men

---

[63] Cole p 589

were able to rest and shower the next day while greeting some new replacements.

McConahey described a shower as follows: "About 10 miles to the rear a quartermaster detachment had set up a shower-bath unit which all of the men in our battalion were permitted to visit, a few at a time. The temperature was below zero, so we were none too warm as we stripped off our clothes in the undressing tent, even though there was a coal stove in the center. Then we ran into the shower tent, where hot water sprayed from multiple holes in several long pipes. It felt wonderful to scrub up again, but it was a different feeling when we ran back to the dressing tent to dry off and get dressed in the freezing air."[64]

[64] McConahey p 101

Chapter Twenty- Six

Bastogne

The day after Christmas, forces under Patton broke through and relieved Bastogne .

Butch's men maintained their defensive positions in the bitter cold through Dec.30, 1944. That day they moved out at 0845 and cleared the woods in front of them. They also hunted for meat as they " killed deer and caught 8 rabbits. " per Butch's diary entries.

Food eaten by the Third Army troops was consistently boring. The B ration supplied about 70% of the meals. It consisted of some fresh meat, white bread, and coffee. There were sometimes oranges. Men on the battle-line lived on the C ration. It had a canned meat and hash. Also, there was the K ration consisting of processed meat and egg and processed cheese and meat. A new and more popular C ration arrived in November. It had spaghetti and meatballs. It was Army tradition on holidays to provide all the men that could be reached with a pound of turkey, a half-pound of chicken and trimmings.

During January 1945, cold weather dominated the memories of the men who fought the battles. All involved suffered. A man had to hurry to complete his business or he got a frostbitten penis. Oil in engines froze. Weapons froze. Men pissed on them to get them working again. Nights ranged from zero degrees Fahrenheit to minus ten and lower. Men stayed awake through the fourteen-hour night stomping their feet or they froze. The GIs went through worst physical misery than the men of Valley Forge. Washington's troops had tents, fires and warm food. They were not involved in continuous battle. The conditions in the Ardennes area in January 1945 were as brutal as any in history, including the 1815 French and 1941 German retreats from Moscow.[65]

---

[65] Ambrose p372

Chapter Twenty- Seven

1945, A New Year

New Years Day found Butch and his men holding the same position. Second platoon ventured out in the cold to attack a pillbox and get some prisoners. They took 4 prisoners, but got showered by German mortar and artillery fire and ran into mines with 12 men falling casualty with one dead.

January 2– 5 was spent weathering the cold with no movement. The next day word was received to prepare to move north to Bastogne. Leaving at 0130 on foot towards the town Koenigsmacker, they hiked for 7 miles and then were picked up by trucks, spending the cold and cloudy night in Koenigsmacker.

On January 7 at 1200, they moved by truck through cold and snow from Koenigsmacker across the Moselle River, through Luxembourg City and then Lannen , Luxembourg. Butch's men arrived in the Bastogne area at dusk in Protz. Two platoons and a command post were housed there while other elements of the company were housed in another town 5 miles north. Butch's diary notes *"Housing was very SNAFU- - Cold & Snowing. "*

January 8, 1945 brought more cold and snow, but no movement. The temperature this day was a few degrees above zero and the snow was piling high making movement difficult for both the Germans and the Americans.

The next day, January 9, Butch's men moved on at 0130 in trucks to Ardorf where they set up indoors.

Orders had been received for an attack the morning of 9 January involving the 357th, 358th and the 359th. The 358th was to capture the high ground northeast of Bras on the main highway to Bastogne. The Germans were beginning a limited withdrawal, pulling troops from the tip of the Bulge.

The 358th gathered near Rambrouch while the other divisions attacked. The 357th, on the left of the 358th, captured 80 Germans at the crossroads of Berle. The 359th on the right captured Trentelhof by 11 January, overcoming artillery, tanks and nebelwerfers (screaming meemie rockets). They captured 380 prisoners. The Germans retreated to Wiltz to the northeast.

The regiments pushed forward through deep snow and woods, eventually reaching high ground overlooking Doncols. They would find that the German resistance would stiffen here so that the Germans could keep open their routes of retreat to the northeast. Doncols fell 11 January with over 300 prisoners captured.

11 Jan. 1945: *Moved out at 1800 to assembly area in woods near* Bavigne (added by author)_____ *where we had hot meal. Then moved out at 1400 to area in woods near_____ There spending the night- Sacks got there at 2100 Cold & Snow.*

12 Jan. 1945: *Moved out at 0800 attacking through woods to high ground N.E. of Sonlez. Outposted the hill & spent night in this position- No new developments- Cold & Cloudy-*

   While Butch and the 358th were taking the high ground, the 357th attacked Sonlez directly taking several hundred prisoners and valuable intelligence information as Sonlez turned out to be a German regimental command post. They ended up on the outskirts of Bras 5 miles east of Bastogne. After several hours of fighting they took the lower part of Bras.

   13 Jan. 1945: *Moved down into town & took over positions held by B Co. at 1600. Spent night in town. No new developments. Cold & Clear*

14 Jan. 1945: Moved out of town at 1400 to assembly area in woods north of Doncols- Were to make night attack, but plans changed- Spent night in this area -Cold & Clear

Division reports say that the German Bulge was eliminated on 14 January and plans called for attacks northeast towards Germany. As the Division pushed towards Bras, the Germans were making an effort to withdraw as their supply lines were being cut off.

The American assault pushed the Germans out of Bras along the Belgium Luxembourg border and up on the high ground beyond the town into the woods. The village of Bras , Belgium was completely destroyed because the Germans had fought hard to keep the road open here. SS troops were moved up as reinforcements and the Germans fought back with vigor. The Americans eventually took the high ground and 122 German prisoners.

The Americans dressed in their dark summer clothes silhouetted against the winter wonderland made highly visible targets for the Germans. All they had for warmth was one long wool overcoat of WWI vintage.

Pockets of Americans and camouflaged Germans lay intermingled throughout the thickly forested countryside in sub-zero weather, often unaware of each other. The snow was knee deep. "The exchanges around Bras were exceedingly violent. We traded blows , back and forth, not for minutes, but for days. I fired for hours with few pauses between."[66] The 358th continued the attack to the northeast at 0800 and was caught in a heavy crossfire of machine guns, artillery and heavy small arms from Germans who had apparently reinforced during the night and entrenched on the opposite slope. The Americans had to pull back due to the intense fire. A couple of American tanks were casualties this day.

Total battalion casualties on January 15,1945 were listed as heavy with 46 killed and wounded including 6 officers. Butch was one of those officers, pulled to safety by Paul Boehm. His war was over.

15 Jan. 1945 : *Moved out to assembly area this morning at 0700- Jerry was there. I got hit- Left Co at 0800- dressed at 2nd Bn Aid. Stopped off at 1st Bn Aid to see Coyle- later went by Ambulance to 115 Med Evac at Thionville- then to Paris-*

The 358th attacked toward Neiderwampach. After crossing some railroad tracks, the 358th was hit with heavy fire from tanks, artillery and small arms fire. On 15 January, Neiderwampach fell to the First battalion. Oberwampach later fell and resisted intense counterattack.

---

[66] Winebrenner p183

Chapter Twenty- Eight

Hospitalized

Butch would miss the next river crossing on the Our River as the Divison fought its way just short of the Siegfried line again. I think he would have preferred this crossing since it was over ice. The Division pushed near Habscheid, Germany and fought their way pillbox by pillbox. Then the armor pushed through on February 22 , 1945. The Division pushed up the Prum River seizing Binscheid, Holchen and Arzfeld. The 90th Division was relieved on February 25, 1945. They resumed the attack on March 6,1945 and captured Gerostein and Pelm racing on to the Rhine . On March 15, 1945 they crossed the Moselle, River for the second time near Hazenport and reached the Rhine on March 18th.

They crossed the Rhine River near Rheinbollen . On March 28th, they crossed the Main River in assault boats meeting scattered resistance. They raced across Germany through Stockheim,Schlitz,Vacha, and Merkers. Bad Salzungen fell on April 3, 1945. In the salt mines of Merkers, the Reich gold reserves were captured along with stolen art treasures. The Division moved on towards the Czechoslovakian border seizing Hof, a large city that was defended by SS troopers and the remaining Wehrmacht. On April 18th, the 358th Infantry was the first to enter Czechoslovakia. A concentration camp containing Poles, Russians and French was liberated at Flossenberg on April 23. The Division advanced into Czechoslovakia towards Susice. On May 8, 1945, Butch's birthday the war ended with the Division making contact with the Russians over the next few days.

Butch spent February 1945 - April 5, 1945 in the 833rd Convalescent Hospital getting ready to go back into action. In a letter to his father, Butch explains to him that he is ok and that there is nothing to worry about even though he lets it slip that he has had a massive amount of penicillin. It turns out he had a life threatening infection from his wound. He describes getting a machine gun bullet though his left thigh that was a fairly clean puncture that only chipped a tiny piece off of his pelvis bone. He said that he can almost walk at the time of the letter and is ready to get back to complete "unfinished business." He reassures his father " I'm sure they were not aiming at me...those bastards can't hit the side of a barn; they are like you Neil in a shooting gallery. "

On April 13, 1945, Butch left Cheltenham for Warrenton where he spent a week. He picked up mail in Borngrove on April 19th. The next day, he left for the 10th replacement Depot at Lichfield at Feasy Farms Estate. April 26th saw Butch travel to Southhampton where he boarded a boat, crossed the channel and landed in France again on April 30th near LeHavre, France arriving at the 15th reinforcement Depot on May 3, 1945. He was on board a train on May 9th and arrived at the 14th replacement Depot on May 10th. He traveled May 23- May 25th and crossed the Rhine at 0355 . On May 26, 1945, Nurnberg, Germany and the 17th Depot was his destination. He trucked the next day to the 90th Division rear where he was happy to be back in his Division. Butch reported to the personnel office discovering that he had been awarded the D.S.C. and an oak leaf cluster to the Silver Star. Butch was then put in command of C Company. He visited A Co. to pick up his gear and souvenirs that were in good shape. The next day, Butch set his unit up in the town of Schonsee on outpost duty.

Chapter Twenty- Nine

Boys and Their Toys

letter to Captain H.C. Neil from Captain Cud T. Baird III,
14 Jan 1947

" I ran into a Major Peters that said he worked with you on
some kind of sand table project. Told him you hadn't
changed.....you were always tinkering with something. In
combat it was cuckoo clocks and after the war that you built
a brick theater and ran a private railroad."

1945, Butch's Private Railroad Company

1945, Butch Driving his Train

When Butch did talk about the war, he had no problem talking about the summer of 1945, the time after the surrender of the Germans. He talked about the wonderful Germans and others that he worked with. He was in charge of a displaced persons camp. There were refugees and ex-German military. He delighted in talking about the chess tournaments that they had, but he was especially proud of his theater and his train.

1945, Butch's Theater Construction Project

Butch Neil quoted in The Scroll of Phi Delta Theta, March 1957

"As you remember, we were on border duty after the end of the war, and the 1st Bn was located in Oberviechtach, Germany. We had an outpost at Schonsee that was rotated by companies --- one spent every third week here. It was here that I found an old switch engine that had been shot up during the war. We got it fixed up and set up our own railroad system between Schonsee and Oberviechtach to move troops back and forth ---- around 30 miles as I remember. Through help of a former German engineer and fireman and our Service Co. welders, we got the train in running condition and made the first trip down from Schonsee with me at the controls. (First time to run a train). Since it was down grade (steep at that), we made a record run down, mainly because I didn't know how to slow it down. We kept the train going until I got over ambitious and sent the German engineer out on the main line to "steal " me a good first-class coach. It was then that the operating railroad battalion of our army stole my entire train. After that we spent our spare time building a theater in Oberviechtach using materials we managed to liberate from local steel and lumber yards".

In a letter to Ed Singer dated November 5,1946, Butch writes about using German POW labor, three lumber yards of lumber, 96,000 bricks and two or three carloads of cement to build quite a theatre.

On July 16, 1945, Captain Neil was transferred out of the 90th to command "F" Co of the 394th Infantry of the 99th Division in Randersalker, Germany. Shortly thereafter, he left Co. F and was placed in charge of the Eppstusse Displaced Persons camp in Wurzberg.,which was for Russians. A Major DeLesdernier was in charge of the nearby Latvian Displaced Persons camp. Butch said he spent a lot of time over there because the Latvians were more pleasant folks than the Russians. The

Major and the Latvians organized a chess tournament. The Major had been Captain of the West Point Chess Team and felt no one could beat him. Butch gleefully described how the Major was defeated by a 12 year Latvian girl in the final match.

On August 28th, he left Wurzburg and moved to tents near Hammelburg in preparation for the trip home. You went home based on a point system for service. He had his needed 85 points. On September 2, 1945, he left by train to the port of Marseilles, France . Butch was coming home.

Chapter Thirty

Post War

The end of the war saw Butch leave the Army in December 1945 and return to Dallas. He did absolutely nothing for the next three months except "sleep, eat and get fat. " Then he started work with the Vendo Company of Kansas City , Missouri where he was the Western regional sales manager. Vendo was a division of the Coca Cola Company. Butch worked for them for 28 years. He continued to serve his country in the reserves from 1946 -1967. He was the battalion commander of the 359th infantry reserve unit in Dallas.

Butch exchanged numerous letters with old war buddies . He mentioned looking up Paul Boehm in Kansas City. Mr. Boehm had pulled Butch out of the field after the German machine gun nailed him in 1945.

There is more than one poignant letter in his files from a mother or a sister ,who lost a loved one in the 90th, ,mentioning that they had seen he was in the 90th from newspaper articles. They were desperately seeking any information about their loved one. These were soldiers that did not serve with Butch . In one letter , Butch wrote to one soldier who thought he served with Butch:

"I'm sorry that I don't remember you in 1944. That's not unusual however since I tried not to really get to know too much about the men I had to lead in combat. It's hard to lead men into actions that might get them wounded or killed. You continue to wonder if you had done something different you might have saved them. That's one of the hard things about being a combat leader. You will lose some men in most military actions, but it still hurts. "

Chapter Thirty- One

In Her Father's Footsteps

Our quest to hook up with the path of the 358th regiment of the 90th began in earnest on 27 August 2014 when we landed in France at Paris ORD, 70 years and a few days after Margie's father. We had gotten a hint of the hospitality to come from a wonderful French lady back at DFW, who struck up a conversation with us in the waiting area, found out why we were going to France and filled us with anticipation about her country and how much they liked Americans.

We picked up our rental car, plugged in our portable GPS with crossed fingers and smiled when the map of France came into focus. On to the coastal town of Honfleur we drove in a light rain. We circled in round- a-bout after round-a-bout, slowly pulling away from the gravitational pull of Paris. We hated round-a-bouts at first, but grew to like them eventually. The GPS saved many an initial headache. Finally, we were in more rural and peaceful countryside that was much steeper than we expected. We climbed in elevation towards the coast through the verdant countryside with an occasional view down into the Seine River valley and riverside communities. Two and one half hours later we arrived in Honfleur, a favorite of artists for hundreds of years. Parking in Honfleur was a challenge, but we finally parked in a large lot at Du Bassin. We hiked around Honfleur, ate ham omelets and fries and finally drove to our more suburban hotel in Equemauville. The parking lot there was full of cops and police cars and we finally figured out they were having some kind of regional educational gathering much to our relief. We needed a good night's rest.

Our plan was to base in Arromanches, check out the Normandy sights and then work our way exactly on the path of the 90th. However, we realized how close we would pass by Falaise so we chose to beeline for it rather than head there after Le Mans as planned. We drove back roads through many French villages finally arriving at the Montormeil memorial site, a memorial to the Allies (British, French, Poles) on their side of the Falaise gap. Then we drove to Chambois and the other side of the gap where the 359th with the 358th on their flank linked up with the Poles to close the gap. The views down into the valley of destruction were pastoral and peaceful in contrast to the hell the Germans faced 70 years prior. Lt. Neil was in combat here.

We worked our way cross-country to Arromanches , a beachside resort town. We parked on the street near our hotel and climbed three fights of stairs to our room with a view of the harbor. The last flight of stairs was more like a spiral ladder. You had to push your suitcase in front of you. It was a fun and quirky place to stay that we enjoyed a lot. Arromanches still has remnants of the temporary harbor that the allies constructed after D-day.

The next day we took in Ste- Marie- Eglise with it's famous church and visited Utah beach where the 90th landed on D-Day.

Driving back towards Arromanches, we visited Pointe du Hoc and its concrete bunker gun emplacements where the US rangers gallantly scaled the cliffs. It is breathtaking with its views of the beaches and is still pock marked and scarred with large craters from the U.S. shelling and bombing on D-Day.

Next on the way was a visit to Omaha beach. We entered on the west end at Vierville-sur-Mer where there is a monument to the U.S. National Guard troops who landed here on D-Day. The U.S. assembled a floating harbor here and this is actually where Lt. Neil arrived on D-Day + 24. After Omaha beach , we journeyed to the scenic American Cemetery, which sits above Omaha beach where we spent several hours. You have to be cold blooded to not be moved by this place and the sacrifices it represents.

The next day was Sunday and our prime destination was Mont Castre and Hill 122. On the way, we stopped for a brief visit at the German Cemetery with its somber black crosses. German mothers made sacrifices also.

This was all hedgerow country, but the hedgerows have different species today. One can imagine how difficult it was to fight from field to field. We traveled through Carentan, Baupte , St- Jores and Lithaire adjacent to Hill 122. Today, Hill 122 is a forested park with recreation for families like picnicking, hiking, biking and fishing in a spring fed pool at an old quarry site. The small mountain had been a quarry for regional stone back to the 1800's. We drove up as far as we could and parked in a gravel parking area. From there, we hiked up a narrow dirt trail past the fishing pool that was lined with friendly Sunday afternoon fishermen.

The trail gets very steep and traverses through a jungle of river birches and ferns. You finally emerge out the top and find yourself at an observation point that looks back down on Lithaire. The Germans had views all the way to the coast from here. It was the site of a Roman fortress in the time of Caesar. Lt. Neil was not in combat here, but it is hallowed ground for the 90th Division.

We drove through Periers with its beautiful monument, St-Lo, St-Hilaire –du- Harcouet, La Doree, Levare, La Butte, Mayenne and on to Le Mans. The terrain was hilly and steep.

We found the village of St- Suzanne near Le Mans and think we found the crossroads where Lt. Neil's platoon took the German tank column in the style of Wild West train robbers. There has been a lot of development in this suburban metropolitan area and there is not a lot of WWII history awareness here. In 1944, Lt. Neil's platoon held German POW's in a village café. During his 1972 trip to France, Butch found this café again and the proprietor was the son of the 1944 owner. The son had been a small child during the war and remembered the event well. Butch's group received warm hospitality from the village. In 1944, they had stacked all the captured German equipment at the café. In 1972 Butch was presented with a souvenir from that pile of captured equipment…a German gas mask.

Our next goal was Chartres via some interesting country lanes over hill and over dale. We would have swung up towards Falaise at this point if we had been chronologically following the 90th but since we had already been there we were able to wander on the way to where we spent the night . We were able to leisurely enjoy the historic city and cathedral. I think the 90th must have passed by here fairly fast because Lt. Neil had no photos of Chartres. The next destination of the 90th was Fontainebleau so we drove on to the famous country escape for French kings. The town center is very narrow and tight. We found Patton Place, a small traffic isle dedicated to the XX Corps under General Patton.

From Fontainebleau, the 90th raced by truck towards Reims and we traveled on the same course over the flat plains that rise in elevation as you approach Reims.

Our hotel in Reims was right on the Canal de'l' Aisne a'la Marne where Butch's 358th regiment, Co. A guarded bridges. We visited Reims Cathedral, a short walk away where Butch took many pictures. Reims , a beautiful city, was where we were able catch our breath after the long drive up the plains east of Paris. It was not hard to imagine the 358th doing the same thing 70 years prior.

1944, Reims Cathedral as photographed by Lt. Neil

We then drove towards our next stopping point that was
Thionville, France. We traveled via Verdun ,St.Hilaire le
Grande, Spincourt, Mont- Bonvillers and ultimately Mairy-
Mainville. The first part of this trip was through the WWI
battleground area. This flat and rolling area would have
looked comfortable to North Texas boys as the land looked a
lot like the land north of Dallas, south of the Red River. For
the last legs near Mairy, we drove down obscure back road
lanes and only saw the occasional farmer We had to pull
over once to let a tractor pass on what was basically a one-
lane track. GPS is liberating as we were on roads not shown
on our Michelin maps.

Mairy was a prime goal since Lt. Neil's unit had a famous encounter here with another armored column. It was especially important to find Mairy to fulfill a void in Lt. Neil's own return trip back to France in the 1970's. He took his wife and traveled with some close friends to find some of these same places. In his diary from that trip (he loved to record things), we read of his frustration of not finding Mairy. Well, they found Mairy and then they found Mairy and Mairy again, but just not the right one. You see there are villages all over France named Mairy. They gave up after checking out a Mairy that was in Belgium. I guess he got mixed up after the whirlwind drive up the plains and it was 30 years later.

In 2014, I had a tool Butch did not have and that was Google. I found Mairy after Mairy also. I finally zoomed in on a Mairy that seemed to be in the right region from my readings. I zoomed in on the village until I could read street names and found one called Rue Du 8 Septembre 8, 1944. I knew this was the right Mairy…Mairy-Mainville. (each Mairy is called Mairy-_____ after the next large nearby community. This one was the Mairy near Mainville). 8 September 1944 was the date on one of Lt. Neil's Silver Star citations. It was the date they liberated this town. Thank you Google.

When we arrived in Mairy- Mainville, we knew we were standing where this battle took place from photos Butch had taken. Little had changed in 70 years. It is a quiet village with orchards , a run down ancient church and barking dogs. The stonewalls along the road look as described by Butch in his diary. There was also another street named Rue De La' 90 eme 90th Division D' Infanterie. Butch, you can check this off your list. Your daughter got here for you.

Above Mairy-Mainville, the land starts to rise in elevation as you exit the flatter plains below. All the way to Thionville , it feels like the lower elevations of Colorado or Montana....like you are approaching a mountain range. Many of the roads are steep with dramatic drop-offs . (in the eyes of a flatlander).

We finally arrived at the L'Horizon hotel, which is right about where the 358th regiment camped in 1944. We would be in considerably more comfortable quarters. This hotel is just down the road from the Guentrange Maginot Fort that today is a museum open on Wednesdays and Saturdays as of this writing. There is WWII film footage of the 90th shelling Thionville from this location.

The 90th Division historian had recommended to Margie, Lt. Neil's daughter that we let the hotel owners know why we were in Thionville because he said the proprietor had some knowledge of Koenigsmacker. We had planned to do this, but gave no advance notice because we did not want to really bother anyone. I was confident that I could find everything since I had a satellite image and detailed directions to the fort. (thank you again Google) We figured that we would confirm our information about where Ft. Koenigsmacker was located and go about our business . Margie introduced herself to Anne Marie Speck at the hotel desk and explained who her father was. She asked us to wait a while and said her husband was away, but she had called him and he was on his way back to the hotel. Meanwhile, Anne Marie handed us an illustrated comic history book entitled "This Fort is Ours" and we sat in their bar to thumb though it. Of course it was about the battle to conquer Ft. Koenigsmacker. Obviously, these guys knew a bit about Koenigsmacker.

Jean Pascal Speck arrived and immediately informed Margie that he knew specifically all about her father Lt. Neil, and his actions at the fort. We were not expecting this and enjoyed chatting with him in his hotel bar. He said he would like to take us to the Fort the next day after he rearranged his schedule.

The next morning, Jean Pascal drove us to the location of the Cattenom River Crossing of the 358th. There is a beautiful marker there in tribute to the event. On the way, we stopped and photographed another Maginot line fort on this side of the river.

As we were visiting the village of Basse -Ham and photographing the church there, Jean Pascal related a funny story about his use of the automatic transmission while driving in the U.S..........which mirrored my recent discomfort with the manual transmission of our rental.

We drove up the farm road to the fort entry road that is a gravel road. I thought back to conversations that I had years ago with my father –in- law when I asked him if he had ever been back to Fort Koenigsmacker. He said that they did find the fort in the 70's, but it was an ordeal. They got to what he thought was the location, but it was totally wooded. He found a farmer that pointed out the location, but told them it was an area that the military controlled and it was off limits. I know that he parked along the road and then ignored the no trespassing signs as the second invasion by Butch Neil commenced. He described climbing up the hill and fighting his way through thick woods. He found a relic German helmet in the fork of a tree still sitting there since the war. I know he found some elements of the fort, but it was way too overgrown for him to really orient himself. But, he knew he was in the area and he had made a necessary pilgrimage to pay tribute to those that fell.

What Butch did not know and we learned was that the French military had tied up this acreage for their use since the war. Only recently, a French organization, the Moselle 1944 group has obtained the right to clean up the fort and restore it as a historic site. They have a plan in place and cleaned up a small portion and created a small parking area adjacent to the fort's shelter point #4.. There is a monument to the 90th and fund-raising is ongoing for the restoration.

We drove in past the original steel entry gates and down a gravel road flanked by rising dirt and thick woods on either side. We parked in the cleared parking area that is the original vehicle parking area in front of (south side) shelter point #4. The underbrush has been removed on this side of shelter point #4. Imprints from the trees that were removed are etched into the concrete on the side of the fort. We nosed around this area and then moved on down between the West Barracks and the Gun Battery. We climbed up steps like a pre-Columbian ruin at Tulum…only this one still had the vines growing around it. After you reached the top, you could see the four gun turrets. There was lots of underbrush. In 1944, Lt. Neil and Lt. Ross yanked a vent cover off a vent and poured gas and grenades down it. In 2014, Lt. Neil's daughter wandered through the underbrush to the edge of the battery squinting for a view to the river. She stumbled on an obstruction. Reaching into the brush , she grasped the object and raised it up. It was a vent cover complete with bullet holes. I strongly feel Butch was with us at Fort Koenigsmacker that day .

2014, Margie Neil Johnston, Butch's
daughter holds bullet riddled vent

Coming down off the Battery, we walked east according to my compass. We stumbled through crisscrossing fields of barbed wire still in place since the war. Art Deco inspired galvanized fence posts are also still in place 70 years later. I believe we rounded Shelter point 10 and then headed north a bit. We had to detour around many downed trees that blocked the easy pathways as we forged our own trails. Jean Pascal was a good sport as we had to crawl under many downed trees. I think we pushed him deeper into the campus of the fort than he had been in some time. We went deep enough that we became a little disoriented. It was getting late in the day so we started thinking about getting back to our stating point. We used the compass a few times to make sure we were headed somewhat westerly. We eventually, after swinging way east, rounded what I believe was the rounded form of the armored outpost at shelter point 4. We came down a steep slope to the main entry road several hundred yards down from where we had parked. We had done an etch a sketch circle of a small part of this vast fortress campus. It was a dangerous and exhilarating Indiana Jones experience. This place should be restored and made accessible to the general public, but we felt honored to have seen it in this raw state. We hope to come back with flashlights and machetes and spend a couple of full days seeing the entire campus.

Anne Marie and Jean Pascal Speck treated us like family. It is a shame Butch did not meet them in 1972. He would have enjoyed a good cocktail hour in their company.

That night we sat down at the bar of the hotel with Jean Pascal and chatted some more. After a while, he strolled over to an easel and pulled off a cloth from it unveiling an oil painting by famed artist Britt Taylor Collins. It is entitled " Taking Fire to Ft. Koenigsmacker". It depicts two "Tough Hombres" rising to the fort with a Jerry can. It is tribute to the collective bravery of the 358th regiment that day depicting the moment Lt. Ross and Lt. Neil grabbed the Jerry cans full of gas.

This was truly an emotional moment in the trip orchestrated by Jean Pascal. An interview was attempted with the daughter of Lt. Neil. As anyone who knows my wife can figure, this was a bad idea as she can be a bit sentimental at times. Every question just brought more tears. Of course, Jean Pascal had tears. He is French! I am sure that I remained dry eyed. I am a Texan. However something did apparently irritate my eyes. I do have some family lineage to Louisiana. Must be some darn French blood. The interview had to be rain delayed, but Margie finally completed it and a nice article appeared in the local newspaper about her pilgrimage. The entire area had a 70th anniversary celebration in November as a tribute to the few remaining living vets.

2014, Fort Koenigsmacker, West Barracks

We cannot say enough about the hospitality of the Specks and the L'Horizon Hotel. It definitely should be a destination for anyone with connections to the 90th.

Reims was our destination again and we enjoyed more time in that city and then on past famed WWI battleground Chateau -Thierry through Lizy-sur- Oureq and on to Mauregard , a rural suburb of Paris where we stayed in a jewel of a hotel owned by a family that was on old family land lost during the French revolution and regained back over the years by the family. It was bittersweet to leave France the next day.

Margie and Chris Johnston at Moselle River monument for the 90th Division at Cattenom, France, 2014

Chapter Thirty- Two

Final Muster, 1997

A patriot to the end Harris C. Neil died on the fourth of July, 1997. It is worth noting that he was born on May 8th which was the day that WWII officially ended. (V.E. day) His historic accomplishment at Koenigsmacker near the WWI battlefield of Verdun concluded on November 11, which was the same day in 1918 that WWI ended. (Armistice Day). George Patton would have said that Butch Neil was a man of destiny.

Colonel H.C. Neil was laid to rest with a formal honor guard ceremony at Calvary Hill Cemetery in Dallas, Texas to a mournful final taps and overhead missing man flight. From a 1995 letter to Butch from Jim Barkalon, a member of his WWII Co. A, 1st platoon we read:

"This is not intended as flattery , but the truth. You are the only officer I ever served with who I respected for their courage, bravery, and dedication to their men. May the Almighty bless you." He would be dearly missed by all.

BIBLIOGRAPHY

Ambrose, Stephen, Citizen Soldier ,New York, Simon & Shuster, 1997

Barnes, Captain Harry B., The Operations of the 1st Battalion, 358th Infantry, 90th Infantry Division at Fort Koenigsmacker North of Thionville , France, 9-11 November 1944 (Rhineland Campaign) , Advanced Infantry Officers Course (AIOC) of the Academic Department of the Infantry School, Ft. Benning Georgia

Bryan, Lt. Col. Charles B., Battle History Third Battalion 358th Infantry (Czechoslavakia, 1945)

Bradley, Gen. Omar N., A Soldier's Story, New York, Henry Holt and Co.,1951

Colby, John, War From The Ground Up, Austin, Texas : Nortex Press, 1991

Cole, Hugh M. , The Lorraine Campaign, Atlanta, Georgia, Whitman Publishing, LLC, 2012

Foster, Hugh, Lt Col (USA, Ret.) historian., article *The Infantry Organization for Combat WWII* ,April 26, 2000 (http://www.trailblazersww2.org/history_infantrystructure. htm)

Huss, Pierre J., " This Fort is Ours ", "Cosmopolitan Magazine", May 1945

Kemp, Anthony, The Unknown Battle, Metz 1944, Briarcliff Mamor, N.Y., 1981

Mayot Enterprises, " The Attack on Fort Koenigsmacker", privately published (booklet), Eagle Lake Minn., 1977

McConahey, William M., M.D., Battalion Surgeon, privately published Rochester, Minnesota, 1966, 1998

Rottman, Gordon L., WWII River Assault Tactics, Osprey Publishing, Oxford, U.K., 2013

Ryan, Cornelius, The Longest Day, New York: Simon and Schuster, 1959

U.S. Army, Peragimus , "We Accomplish: A Brief History of the 358th Infantry ", Weiden, Germany: Ferdinand Niccki, 1945. 56 p. # 603-358.1945 (booklet)

Von Luck, Col. Hans, Panzer Commander, The Memoirs of Colonel Hans Von Luck, New York , Dell Publishing, 1989

Winebrenner, Hobert & McCoy, Mike, Bootprints, Albion IN, Camp Comamajo Press 2005

Appendix 1

US Army Operational Units and leadership level

Army (2- 5 Corps) 200,000 – 450,000 men: Four Star General
Corps (2-5 Divisions) 90,000 men: ....Lt. General
Division (3 + regiments) 10,000- 20,000 men: Major General
Regiment (3 + Battalions) 3,000 – 5,000 men: Colonel
Battalion (3-5 Companies) 500 -600 men: Lt. Col.
Company (3-4 Platoons) 100- 200 men: Captain
Platoon (3-4 Squads) 40 men :   Lieutenant
Rifle Squad 6-12 men: Sergeant

The Infantry Battalion was made up of three rifle companies ,
a headquarters company and a heavy weapons company.
Headquarters Company was designated as "HHC". Letters
that ran consecutively through the three battalions of the
regiment designated other companies. Thus 1st battalion
consisted of A,B and C companies (rifle companies) and D
(heavy weapons) while 2nd Battalion contained E,F, and G
companies (rifle companies) and H (heavy weapons) and
3rd battalion contained I,K and L companies (rifle
companies) and M (heavy weapons).

Col. H.C. Neil Jr. 1916 - 1997

Photography Credits and Thanks

All contemporary photos are by Chris Johnston

Family photos from Neil family archives

WWII photos were by Lt. Harris Neil except as noted below:

Photo of M2 Assault Boat by the US Army Signal Corps courtesy National Archives

Maps by Chris Johnston

Front Cover Photo: Steps at Fort Koenigsmacker

Thanks to Norm Richards, historian with the 90th Infantry Division for assistance with retrieval of Morning Reports and to Tyler Alberts for the suggestion to stay at L' Horizon Hotel where we met the Specks.

Special thanks to Ann Marie and Jean Pascal Speck. We are forever indebted.